GENDER, CHRISTIANITY AND AFRICAN CULTURE

GENDER, CHRISTIANITY AND AFRICAN CULTURE

RECLAIMING THE VALUES OF INDIGENOUS MARRIAGE AND FEMALE INITIATION RITES

Jonathan Kangwa

GENDER, CHRISTIANITY AND AFRICAN CULTURE: RECLAIMING THE VALUES OF INDIGENOUS MARRIAGE AND FEMALE INITIATION RITES
by Jonathan Kangwa

© Copyright 2017

SAINT PAUL PRESS, DALLAS, TEXAS

First Printing, 2017.

ISBN-13: 978-1545288191
ISBN-10: 1545288194

Printed in the U.S.A.

*I dedicate this book to my son Malumbo Kangwa,
the little angel,
and to my wife Chileshe
who kept encouraging me to finish this project.
To her I say bravo!
Mwabombeni!*

CONTENTS

ACKNOWLEDGEMENTS

I would like to acknowledge the meticulous assistance I received from Professor Sarojini Nadar of the University of KwaZulu-Natal in South Africa. Professor Nadar made valuable contributions to this project and really helped me to clarify my thinking. I could not have completed this study if she had not guided and motivated me. The research involved was facilitated through a partial grant that I received from the World Mission Council of the Church of Scotland. Some sections in this book were part of the thesis submitted for a Masters degree in Gender and Religion in the School of Religion, Philosophy and Classics at the University of KwaZulu-Natal. More chapters have been included to broaden the scope. I am grateful to all who have, in one way or another, contributed to this project. They are too many to mention by name, but to all of them I offer a heartfelt 'thank you.'

PREFACE

Almost all African societies celebrate marriage and female initiation rites to mark the process of growing up. Initiation rites signal the transition from one stage in life to another. Between the two stages initiates find themselves in 'the camp,' a liminal phase in which they live a secluded existence and are initiated into the mysteries of life.[1] Through initiation rites, they are made aware of positions of power and social relationships in society. The Bemba people of Zambia perform the Chisungu female initiation rites, a ritual process that introduces young women into adulthood. The Bemba also perform marriage rites, initiating bride and bridegroom into married life. Both marriage and Chisungu female initiation rites remain an important source of traditional education on sex and on the social and religious leadership roles played by women in Zambia. However, the different ceremonies are nowadays somewhat modified and shortened. In Bemba traditional society, marriage rites and female initiation rites are related as the seclusion of a girl on reaching puberty is aimed at preparing her for married life (*ukumukusha*).

This study draws on the theoretical insights and critical analyses of anthropologists, sociologists, and theologians who have studied the relations between gender, religion, and African culture, particularly in the last three decades and with a focus on marriage and female initiation rites on the continent. The objective of the study is to offer a gendered analysis of marriage and Chisungu initiation rites among the Bemba people and to retrieve those values of indigenous female initiation rites that can reinforce a critique of patriarchy and promote equality. Patriarchy, rule of the father, is considered as a cause of the low status of women in Africa. Their low status prevents women from making meaningful contributions to society, economically and culturally as well as religiously. It also makes women more vulnerable than men to societal challenges such as climate change and disease, including HIV, AIDS, and cervical cancer.

The study discusses relevant sociological and anthropological conceptual frameworks. It explains the function, form, and practices of indigenous marriage and female Chisungu initiation rites and it reveals the gendered cultural values of these rites, providing details of the symbolic meanings of the ceremonies, the initiation songs, and the sacred marriage emblems (*imbusa*). The study considers how certain gendered cultural values of indigenous marriage and Chisungu initiation rites can be retrieved to promote equality and egalitarianism. Finally, the importance of incorporating values of indigenous marriage and female Chisungu initiation rites into modern-day social, economic, and religio-political practices for the sake of empowering women is explored.

(Footnotes)

1 Victor W. Turner. 1967. The forest of symbols: Aspects of Ndembu ritual. Ithaca NY: Cornell University Press, Victor W. Turner. 1969. The ritual process: Structure and anti-structure. Chicago: Aldine.

CHAPTER ONE

GENERAL INTRODUCTION

1.1 INTRODUCTION

A number of studies on marriage and puberty initiation rites have been carried out by anthropologists, sociologists, historians, and African (women) theologians. The present study builds on the body of work created by these scholars. Audrey Isabel Richards in her dated but excellent book, *Chisungu: A girl's initiation ceremony among the Bemba of Zambia*, provides us with a detailed record of female puberty initiation rites among the Bemba people of Zambia.[1] She argues that the ceremony prepares girls for marriage and a change in status. A woman who has not gone through the ceremony is considered as uncultured (*chitongo*).[2] She reasons that the rites protect girls from the pitfalls of adulthood and enable them to enjoy safe intercourse with their husbands and a safe delivery of their children.[3] She underscores that the ritual bestows on girls the power of fecundity and removes the risks of sex and menstrual blood.[4]

R.M. Kambole in his book, *Ukufunda umwana kufikapo,* provides a detailed description of Bemba marriage and puberty rites in pre-colonial Zambia.[5] He also records songs that were sung during these ceremonies.

Similarly, Y.A. Chondoka in his book, *Traditional marriage in Zambia*, discusses marriage rites in Zambia.[6] More recently, Rasing has researched girls' initiation rites in the context of the urban Roman-Catholic community in Zambia.[7] Her main focus was on establishing the significance of the rites of passage for urban women.[8] She makes the point that, during initiation, girls are taught how to initiate sexual relations with their husbands and actively participate in coitus.[9] Rasing shows that the Chisungu initiation rites remain today the main institution providing instruction on sexuality to Zambian women in rural as well as urban settings, and many of them claim that the values they were taught in initiation school are helpful in the prevention of HIV infection.[10] Rasing laments that the efforts of Catholic missionaries to include *Bana Chimbusa* - tutors in initiation schools - in the teaching of young people about HIV and AIDS have not materialised.[11] Many other studies cover marriage and initiation rites in Zambia, some of them written by Catholic priests and pastors of other churches such as the Seventh Day Adventists. Most of these books are not of a conventional scholarly nature and are aimed at ordinary readers. The above-mentioned works by Richards and Rasing are based on a more academic anthropological approach.

Marriage and female initiation rites belong to the rites of passage. Rites of passage mark the transition from one stage in life to another. They include rituals associated with birth, puberty, marriage, and death. Writing on the Asante people in Ghana, Oduyoye notes that female initiation rites marking the passage from childhood to adulthood[12] are performed by women and that pregnancy is an abomination if it occurs before puberty rites have been performed.

Religion in Africa, particularly Christianity and Islam, has contributed to the transformation of indigenous marriage and female initiation rites.[13] Isabel Apawo Phiri in her book, *Women, Presbyterianism and Patriarchy: Religious experience of Chewa women in central Malawi*, considers the status of women in Chewa culture and describes their struggles for full recognition in society and church.[14] She disapproves of the attitude of Christian missionaries to initiation rites. The missionaries banned such indigenous rituals and replaced them with Christianised initiation ceremonies. Phiri argues that African indigenous female initiation rites should not be condemned out of hand. They have negative aspects as well as positive points that must be upheld.[15] Molly Longwe has conducted a study of initiation rites among the Chewa women of Lilongwe in Malawi[16], focusing on the Christianisation of pre-Christian Chewa initiation rites in the Baptist convention of Malawi. She highlights how indigenous marriage and female initiation rites (*Chinamwali*) dehumanised women in pre-colonial African society. Building on Longwe, Fiedler has studied how Baptist women in southern Malawi perceive both traditional and church initiation rites[17] and concludes that there are liberating as well as oppressive elements in the African initiation rituals.[18]

Contemporary conditions such as the risks of HIV and AIDS, climate change, cervical cancer, and various social challenges have exposed the fact that women in African society are more vulnerable than men. This state of affairs has attracted the attention of scholars to the position of African women and the role that culture and religion have played in their subjugation. Fulata Moyo has analysed ways to inculturate female initiation rites in Malawi today.[19] She highlights that such initiation rites influence female perceptions and practices of sexuality in rural Malawi.[20] She argues that targeting religio-cultural processes among people in Zomba can lead to safer sexual practices and increased gender equality. Moyo's work is a solid contribution to the development of a more empowering sexual education programme by inculturating the strengths of female initiation rites (*chinamwali*) in Malawi.

In the last three decades, similar studies have been conducted in Zambia, focusing on female initiation rites and on the situation of Zambian women in general. Hugo Hinfelaar has written on the Bemba women of Zambia.[21] He shows that in Bemba traditional religion women played social and religious leadership roles as enablers of the domestic cult (*chibinda wa ng'anda*), as initiators of public worship (*kabumba wa mapepo*), and as tutors of the transcendent (*nachibunsa wa chisungu*).[22] He further argues that such female leadership roles were sidelined by the missionaries and later by political leaders in Zambia.[23] In Hinfelaar's view, a great deal of problems among women in Zambia, today, can be attributed to neglect in the past of the original tenets of African traditional religion (ATR). The perception that the vulnerability of women in Zambia to HIV and AIDS is largely due to their loss of the leadership roles they fulfilled in traditional societies, is central to, and will be elaborated on, in this study.

Drawing on Hinfelaar, Kaunda has delved into possibilities to reclaim the feminine image of God in Lesa (God) among Bemba Christian women.[24] He argues that when European Christian missionaries ('white fathers') began to work among the Bemba, they replaced the feminine characteristics of the Bemba God *Lesa* with an all-male concept, thus preventing women from closely associating themselves with the Judeo-Christian God.[25] Using the translatability theory, he argues that reclaiming the feminine image of the Bemba God can empower women and make them see themselves as reflecting the image of the Christian-Judeo God. Extending this argument it may be suggested that the process of reclaiming the feminine image of the Bemba God needs to be accompanied by a revival of those values of the initiation rites that used to pass the perception of a feminine image of God along with the traditional social and religious roles of women from one generation to the next. This suggestion is supported by the link between, on the one hand, social and religious roles played by women and by female initiation rites, and on the other hand, women's ability to deal with contemporary problems such as climate change and the prevalence of cervical cancer, HIV, and AIDS.

A study conducted by the University of Zambia in urban towns reveals that about 87 percent of women undergo initiation rites when they reach puberty and about 78 percent do so prior to marriage. Further, 88 percent of young women between the ages of 19 and 28 years said they would adhere to the teachings provided during female initiation rites.[26] This confirms that marriage and female initiation rites remain a major source of information on sex and married life in Zambia. Previous research on gender and HIV and AIDS in Zambia indicates that gender inequality and patriarchal cultural practices have contributed significantly to the vulnerability of women to HIV and AIDS.[27] Indigenous marriage and female initiation rites were mainly blamed for this.

What goes almost unnoticed in the presently existing body of research, however, is that African indigenous culture also offers values which can be used to critique patriarchy, and hence, to empower women in the context of HIV and AIDS.[28] It is true that the rites contain elements that promote the subjugation of women and these have been identified as the root cause of limitations experienced by Zambian women in any aspect of life. Scholars and activists have called on government, non-governmental organisations (NGOs), the church, and other stakeholders to address harmful practices in African culture. Siwila has examined the views of the United Church of Zambia (UCZ) concerning traditional marriage practices that hinder the prevention of HIV and AIDS.[29] She argues that the UCZ is not doing enough to influence cultural issues such as child marriage and widows' rights to inherit, both of which fuel the spread of HIV in Zambia.[30] She proposes that cultural analysis should serve as a model for the UCZ's dealing with cultural practices that are harmful in the context of HIV and AIDS.[31]

Clearly, much research done on gender, religion, and African culture indicates that culture and religion (in this case Christianity) have, to a large extent, contributed to the subjugation of women in society. Beverly Haddad notes that continued cultural oppression has led to the death of thousands of women through AIDS-related illnesses.[32] She adds that the traditions of the church and lack of analysis of patriarchy and gender injustice have led to a taboo on the discussing of sexuality resulting in women becoming more vulnerable to the HIV epidemic.[33] Isabel Phiri elaborates that this increased vulnerability is caused by differences in physiology, in social and cultural norms, and in economic and power relations between men and women.[34] She emphasises that in traditional marriage and female initiation ceremonies, the sexual education of women and girls is focused on satisfying the sexual needs of their husbands. While sexual satisfaction in marriage is a good thing, a too pertinent stress on the need for women to satisfy men has proved to be problematic in the context of the HIV and AIDS pandemic.

As churches are embarking on the inculturation of female marriage and initiation rites, the work done by scholars belonging to the Circle of Concerned Women Theologians has significantly increased an awareness of both the liberating and the oppressive aspects of initiation rites. However, not much has been written on this subject from a Zambian point of view, creating a gap which this book will attempt to fill. In addition, the available studies have hardly focused on the possibility of reclaiming the traditional social and religious leadership roles of women for the sake of empowering women today, helping them to deal with contemporary challenges such as poverty, climate change, cervical cancer, HIV, and AIDS. This study will provide analyses of marriage and Chisungu female initiation rites among the Bemba people of Zambia, showing how specific values may be of use in present society.

1.2 RESEARCH QUESTION AND OBJECTIVES

1.2.1 RESEARCH PROBLEM AND STATEMENT

Research on gender, Christianity, and African culture in Zambia indicates that patriarchal cultural practices have made women more defenseless when challenged by contemporary issues of poverty, climate change, HIV, and AIDS. Given also that recent research recognizes in African culture values that criticize patriarchy from within resulting in the empowerment of women, this study will investigate which are the specific gendered values in indigenous marriage and Chisungu initiation rites that are worth retrieving and integrating into present-day culture with the aim of strengthening the position of women in Zambia.

1.2.2 RESEARCH QUESTION

What gendered cultural values may be reclaimed from indigenous marriage and female Chisungu initiation rites that can motivate the criticizing of patriarchy and empower women in the context of contemporary challenges such as poverty, climate change, HIV, and AIDS?

1.2.3 RESEARCH HYPOTHESIS

The hypothesis on which the present research is based is that values contained in indigenous marriage and female Chisungu initiation rites among the Bemba people of Zambia offer possibilities for a criticism of patriarchy leading to the empowerment of women in the face of present-day challenges such as poverty, climate change, HIV, and AIDS.

1.2.4 KEY QUESTIONS

The study will seek to answer the following key questions:

- What do indigenous marriage and female Chisungu initiation rites entail?
- What are the gendered cultural values of indigenous marriage and female Chisungu initiation rites?
- How can gendered cultural values of marriage and female Chisungu initiation rites be retrieved to be applied to the empowering of women faced with contemporary challenges such as poverty, climate change, HIV, and AIDS?
- How can integrating and inculturating the values of indigenous marriage and female Chisungu initiation rites in Zambian society empower women in the present-day context of poverty, climate change, HIV, and AIDS?

1.2.5 RESEARCH OBJECTIVES

The objectives of the study are:

- To explain the function, form, and practices of indigenous marriage and female Chisungu initiation rites.
- To identify the gendered cultural values of indigenous marriage and female Chisungu initiation rites.
- To demonstrate how gendered cultural values of indigenous marriage and female Chisungu initiation rites can be retrieved in the context of contemporary challenges such as poverty,

climate change, HIV, and AIDS.

- To assess the importance of integrating the values of indigenous marriage and Chisungu initiation rites into present day Zambian culture for the purpose of empowering women faced with challenges such as poverty, climate change, HIV, and AIDS.

1.2.6 THEORETICAL FRAMEWORK

A number of theories are used in this study. Feminist cultural hermeneutics, as developed by Musimbi Kanyoro, enables the author to review cultural practices and rituals to establish whether they offer valuable possibilities for the empowerment of women.[35] African feminist cultural hermeneutics aims to critique and reclaim aspects of African culture.[36] It exposes harmful elements and injustice in society and its striving is extended to include the culture and practices of the church. Christianity in Zambia and in particular the church as an institution is made up of people who are predominantly Africans and who believe in African culture. Thus, African cultural values and beliefs have a bearing on how Africans perceive Christianity and how they interpret the Bible. In this context, there is a need to scrutinise church culture and define its liberative potential.

Kanyoro affirms the need to reclaim culture through the theology of inculturation, but stipulates the importance of analysing the reclaimed culture or cultural values to determine whether they will indeed bring more justice and greater dignity to women's lives.[37] In the midst of today's challenges, Africans look to cultural resources for answers. The author argues that building on indigenous traditions that may empower women facing contemporary problems are a good starting point. Hence, a feminist cultural hermeneutics is important for this study. So is a process of talking about and testing the seemingly relevant information that we collect in our pursuit of increased empowerment of women.

The study also draws on social change theory. Generally, changes in cultural and religious beliefs and practices can be attributed to social factors. Scholarly studies of processes involving social change show that societies tend to create boundaries protecting them from outsiders.[38] In a community where rituals such as initiation rites are performed, these serve to confirm initiates as members of the group and to demarcate the community's different components. Rituals express the significance of beliefs and validate them. Hence, initiation rites seal the incorporation of initiates into the wider society.

Reeler and Lumbwe list three types of change, namely, emergent change, transformative change and projectable change.[39] These forms of change are an inherent part of the development of human beings. First, society may experience emergent change when people in daily life, as individuals and as members of families or communities, learn and adopt new beliefs and practices. The process may take place consciously or unconsciously. Second, people may as a result of some crisis adopt new beliefs and practices. For example, a community that suffers from the effects of climate change or of high levels of unemployment, poverty, or disease, looks for beliefs and practices that can assist in efforts to survive. In the third place, people may adopt new beliefs and practices through projectable change. This involves consciously undertaking a well-planned process of change.

Change is inevitable. Societies and institutions experience at all times both change and continuity in their beliefs and practices. Due to external factors such as colonialism and the influence of western civilization, migration, globalisation, and secularisation, the social fabric of societies may change dramatically in some respects while remaining constant in others. Concerning marriage and female initiation rites, there is no doubt that cultural insights and practices of the Bemba people of Zambia have changed over time and have been modified under the influence of forms, structures, and qualities of western cultures as well as the cultures of other African tribes encountered by the Bemba. Migration or change of geographical location often results in the mixing of beliefs and cultures. In addition to migrating internationally or locally in the context of social mobility, Zambians tend to move from rural to urban areas.[40] This affects their outlook on life and on the world. Hence, as their living patterns change, cultural practices are also transformed to suit new situations. Processes of social, political, and religious change are strongly impacted by cultural change. People who have acquired a western education tend to identify with western life styles, expressing a new self-image, different personal standards, and the attainment of a higher status in society. At the same time, they are not completely detached from their traditional African background and culture. As a result, they often adopt Christian practices that mix African culture with western secular beliefs. This has contributed to changes in, for example, indigenous forms of marriage and female Chisungu initiation rites which are nowadays performed in a shortened form.[41]

1.2.7 METHODOLOGY

This study has for its data collection employed both empirical and non-empirical methodologies. The researcher attended marriage rituals and part of Chisungu initiation rites in Mpika, Chinsali, and Kitwe districts between 2006 and 2014. Structured interviews were conducted with initiates and tutors of marriage and female initiation schools (banachimbusa). Oral interviews were found to be relevant to this particular study. As Denis observes, oral interviews offer opportunities to "uncover and to improve the knowledge of the past."[42]

A literature survey on marriage and female initiation rites was conducted.

The data collected is analysed on the basis of information resulting from the literature survey, thereby, the social change theory, feminist cultural hermeneutics and inculturation theory[43] were used as heuristic tools. The values of feminist and gender discourse, religion, and African culture are brought into a 'conversation' with each other with the purpose of isolating those aspects of African culture and religion that may be life-giving to girls and women. Fiedler stipulates the importance of analysing and integrating the positive values of initiation rites to strengthen women's resistance against male domination.[44] In that process, she points out elements that could increase the oppression of women should be cast aside.[45] Hinfelaar argues that contemporary problems including illnesses that mostly affect women may be attributed to the past neglect of leadership roles played by women in African traditional religion (ATR).[46] He proposes the inculturation of initiation rites where women serve as leaders and priestesses.[47] The present study suggests a similar approach with the aim of empowering women by reclaiming their roles in traditional marriage and initiation rituals of which the positive values should be revived as part of contemporary social culture.

1.3 CONCLUSION

This introductory chapter describes the background and motivation for the study. Research on aspects of gender, Christianity and African culture in Zambia has largely blamed indigenous marriage and female initiation rites for the marginalisation of women. The present study seeks to analyse how African marriage and initiation rites may yet prove to be of considerable help in attempts by contemporary society to empower women. Chapter one briefly discusses the available body of literature on gender, Christianity, and African culture, showing that, thus far, little attention has been paid to the possibilities offered by traditional marriage and female Chisungu initiation rites as resources for dealing with patriarchy and other contemporary challenges. Despite being banned by missionaries and colonial authorities, African marriage and female initiation rites continue to be practised by Zambian women today. As this study will make clear, even in their contemporary shortened versions these rites remain an important and culturally accepted source of information about sexuality and the roles and status of women.

CHAPTER TWO

SOCIOLOGY, ANTHROPOLOGY, CULTURE, AND GENDER: CONCEPTS AND THEORIES

2. 1 INTRODUCTION

Almost all African societies punctuate the process of growing up with initiation rites. Initiation rites mark the transition between two different stages in life and one of their core responsibilities is to guide young people from childhood to adulthood. The rituals remain an important feature of most African societies although they are nowadays performed in shortened forms.[1]

Initiation rites are transition rites taking a person from a lower level to a higher level in society or perhaps from an 'earlier' to a 'later' stage in life. Between the two levels is the 'camp,' the liminal phase in which initiates live in isolation and are introduced to the mysteries of life. La Fontaine shows that the rites have a social meaning and consist in symbolic actions.[2] The rites educate initiates on different positions of power and social relations in the community. The Bemba people of Zambia perform both marriage and female Chisungu initiation ceremonies whereby the ritual process dramatically creates a liminal period between childhood and adulthood.[3] Because marriage and female initiation rites are about the transition between different stages in life, it is of interest to explain some related gender, sociological, and anthropological concepts and theories.[4]

2.2 SOCIOLOGY

The origin of sociology as a discipline is attributed to Auguste Comte (1798-1857) who defined sociology as the study of interaction between institutions such as the family, educational, religious, and developmental institutions and the ways in which transformation of societies occurs.[5] As an academic discipline, sociology is the study of social institutions and human behaviour in society or groups. Society, as Kibera and Kimoti note, is a "congregation of human beings who share a common cultural heritage in terms of language and inhabitancy of a specific geographical region."[6] The survival of society is dependent on its ability to produce children and to induct them into that society's specific ways. Members of the society are expected to fit and operate in social systems such as family, religion, government, and economic structures. Sociologically, every individual in society has a specific role to play within the existing social systems and to do so adhering to the defined values of the society.

Sociology as a discipline has evolved over time. The French Revolution led to the disorganisation of European society and the establishment of democratic practices. In addition, technological advancement led to industrialisation and to the greater social mobility of people. This mobility affected family units. Scholars such as Auguste Comte, Herbert Spencer, Emile Durkheim, and Max Weber believed that the discipline of sociology could assist in the re-establishment of order in society.[7]

Comte identifies two broad fields of sociological study, namely, social statics and social dynamics. Social statics is the study of the different institutions that form the foundation of society such as the family, economics, the church, government, and so on. The study of social dynamics focuses on how societies develop and change over time. The concept holds that societies have moved through certain stages of development from the primitive ages onwards, to reach the advanced state of today's society. Each stage represents a phase of intellectual development.[8] However, not all societies go through the same stages as some cultures borrow materials and ideologies from other cultures in which case development results from a process of diffusion.[9]

Herber Spencer (1820-1903), a British sociologist, describes progress as the result of societies' journey through various socio-cultural stages, from the primitive tribalism of homogeneous groups to large-scale industrial heterogeneous societies. Spencer was a social evolutionist who likens society to an organism of which the parts function harmoniously to form an integrated whole. Spencer was strongly influenced by Charles Darwin's theory of evolution which states that some species become extinct because they fail to adapt to a changing environment. In that same way, Spencer thought, would weak societies perish and strong ones survive?[10]

Emile Durkheim (1858-1917), a French sociologist, considers society as a reality that exists independently from the individual human being. The existence of the society is reflected in its beliefs, codes of human conduct, and ideals. Durkheim coins the theory of social cohesion. He argues that, the higher the degree of social cohesion, the less likely it is that individuals commit suicide except in cases of over-integration. He identifies three types of suicides. First, altruistic suicide which results from the over-integration of an individual into a group. Rigid rules, norms, and codes of conduct may lead one to commit suicide for the sake of group goals. Second, egoistic suicide which results when a person has become alienated from his group. The person becomes self-centred and lacks emotional support from the group. The third type of suicide is anomic suicide which occurs when there is a lack of defined roles or guidelines to regulate the behaviour of members of a society. In such a case, a person finds no meaning in life and decides to commit suicide. Durkheim further identifies two types of societies, the mechanical society and the society that is characterised by organic solidarity. Mechanical societies are primitive (folk) societies in which people relate to each other in almost every aspect of their existence and have deep feelings. An example of this is the family relations in modern societies. Organic (modern or industrial) societies are held together by a web of relationships based on contracts.[11]

Max Weber (1864-1920), a German sociologist and economist, defined sociology as a science that attempts to interpret social action to arrive at a causal explanation of its effects. For Weber, social action is all about human behaviour to which acting individuals attach subjective meanings.[12] In his publication, "The Protestant ethic and spirit of capitalism" (1904), Weber argues that religious ideas impact economic activities. Christian Protestantism emphasises that there is no conflict between material possessions and salvation. Material success is by Weber seen as a sign of God's blessings. On the other hand, in Weber's view, Catholicism emphasises repentance of sin and does not emphasise material possessions, wealth, ambition, and success on earth.[13]

Weber came up with the bureaucratic theory of leadership or management. This theory deals with the organisation and co-ordination of human activities on the basis of rules, qualifications and competences, and positions of authority (scalar command), rather than on the basis of persons of authority. Thus, there is no room for emotional concerns or individual differences. Three different styles of leadership are identified: the charismatic, the traditional, and the bureaucratic legal authority. Under charismatic domination, authority rests on extraordinary and magnetic qualities which are by both leader and followers believed to be inspired by the supernatural power. Under traditional domination a leader is bound by custom which sanctions their right to the arbitrary exercise of their will. Under legal domination the leader authority rests on generalised rules. Weber believes that capitalism will continue to widen the gap between rich and poor and eventually lead to socialism.[14]

Karl Marx (1818-1883), German as well, was not a sociologist, although his ideas have influenced modern sociology. In The Communist Manifesto (1848), Marx states that societies are divided in two classes: the "haves" or the bourgeoisie, and the "have nots" or the proletariat. Members of the bourgeoisie own the means of production: factories, machines, and capital, while the proletarians are the workers who have nothing but their labour to sell at prices set by the capitalists. Marx sees society as infested with conflicts of an economic nature. These conflicts force society to move from one stage to another. For example, the French Revolution forced society from feudalism and autocracy to the introduction of more democratic institutions with the people voting to elect their representatives in government.[15]

Sociology, in short, is the scientific study of human behaviour in groups called society. The origin of sociology as a discipline can be traced back to the nineteenth century when the French Revolution and the industrial revolution, especially in Britain, disturbed the status quo and caused social disorder in society. Scholars proposed different strategies to re-establish social balance.

2.3 ANTHROPOLOGY

Anthropology is a partly biological and partly social science discipline. It encompasses many study directions that can be classified under various academic disciplines. It belongs, in short, to a number of academic disciplines or sub-disciplines that are related, but distinct. These include physical anthropology, cultural and social anthropology, archaeology, linguistics, and applied anthropology.[16] The distinction between cultural and social anthropology becomes clear only after separating culture from social structures. Many anthropological studies focus on physical anthropology and on subjects of a sociocultural nature. Among the theorists of social and cultural anthropology we find functionalists, structuralists, and symbolic theorists among others. Conrad Phillip Kottak notes:

> Anthropology is the holistic and comparative study of humanity. It is the systematic exploration of human biological and cultural diversity. Examining the origins of, and changes in, human biology and culture, anthropology provides explanations for similarities and differences. The four subfields of general anthropology are (socio-)cultural, archaeological, biological, and linguistic. All consider variation in time and space. Each also examines adaptation – the process by which organisms cope with environmental stresses.[17]

Anthropology and sociology are related. Generally, anthropologists tend to emphasise fieldwork, holistic perspectives, and comparative approaches. These are not particularly stressed in sociological studies. Instead, sociologists employ survey research as an important tool in their studies. If they are dealing with literate respondents, survey researchers use questionnaires that respondents fill in. Sociologists study samples on the basis of which they make inferences relating to larger groups. Due to the diversity of social life in modern nations, anthropologists will on occasion also adopt certain survey procedures, although they strive to retain the intimacy and first-hand investigation that are characteristic of ethnography.[18]

Historically, anthropologists have concentrated mainly on primitive or pre-literate peoples. Studies on literate, modern, and industrial societies started after 1930 as Kibera and Kimoti rightly record. Physical anthropology deals with the origins of human beings and with variations of the human species. It includes the study of race. Social and cultural anthropology on the other hand focus on the study of culture and ways of life among pre-literate communities throughout the world.

Biological or physical anthropology refers to human biological diversity in time and space. It is concerned with the investigation of human evolution as revealed by fossil records (palaeo-anthropology), human genetics, human growth and development, human biological plasticity (the body's ability to adapt to, for example, heat, cold, and altitude), and the biology, evolution, and behaviour of primates.[19]

Linguistic anthropology studies language in its social and cultural contexts across space and over time. It makes inferences about universal features of language, it reconstructs ancient languages by comparing their contemporary descendants and aims to discover perceptions and patterns of thought in different cultures. Historical linguistics studies the variation of language over time such as changes in sound, grammar, and vocabulary. Socio-linguistics concentrates on relationships between social and linguistic variations. The culture of a group is generally learned by its members rather than inherited through biological means. Human beings have the ability to learn, to think in symbols, to use language for expressing themselves, and to employ tools to organise their lives and deal with the environment.[20]

Anthropology has contributed significantly to an understanding of humankind by describing and explaining similarities and differences between groups. It has also illuminated the meaning of human actions in their specific socio-cultural contexts. Several anthropologists have in their field studies concentrated on and analysed religious phenomena. Among these are Victor Turner, Elizabeth Colson, and Thera Rasing all of whom have done extensive fieldwork in Zambia.

2.4 CULTURE AND RELIGION

Culture refers to distinctive patterns of ideas, beliefs, and norms that characterize the way of life of a society or a group and the relations between its members. Culture consists of the traditions and customs transmitted through learning. These traditions and customs are governed by the beliefs and behaviours of the people who are exposed to them.[21] Through a process called enculturation human beings learn the traditions and customs that prevail in a particular society. Cultural traditions also include those habits and opinions developed over time that refer to proper and improper behaviour in a society. They define what, in a specific situation, one ought to do or what one should refrain from doing.[22] Religion and culture are interrelated. Religion can be defined as a cultural universal which consists of beliefs and behaviours concerning supernatural beings and forces. Religion has functions of an emotional, social, political, and ecological nature.

In Africa, religion and culture are interwoven. One cannot separate culture from religion or religion from culture. Religio-culture establishes and maintains social control. To do so it promotes a series of moral and ethical beliefs that are accompanied by real and imagined rewards and punishments, an awareness of which is internalised by individuals. Religio-culture uses mobilisation of its members for collective action as one way of achieving social control. Religion can also promote change.

Religion and culture are social constructs. In Africa, people use magic to try and influence outcomes over which they have no technical or rational control. Religion may provide comfort and psychological security when there are crises such as a famine or pestilence. Rituals play an important role in the religious life of Africans. Ritual involves formal, unchanging, earnest acts that require people to play an active role in a social collective. For example, rites of passage mark changes in social status, age, place, or social conditions. Collective rituals are cemented by *communitas*, a feeling of intense fellowship and solidarity.[23]

As a social construct culture can be regarded as a "complex whole which includes knowledge, beliefs, arts, morals, law, custom, and any other capabilities and habits acquired by man as a member of society."[24] It enables people to share organised life in groups called society. While human beings have the privilege of sharing life with animals, including dogs, goats, chickens etc., culture is distinctive to humans. Cultural learning depends on the unique use of symbols and signs that have no necessary or natural connection to the things they signify or for which they stand. Cultures apply specific systems of symbolic meaning. A symbol is a verbal or non-verbal expression within a particular language or culture that comes to stand for something else. There is usually no obvious natural or necessary connection between the symbol and that which it symbolises. Among the Bemba people of Zambia, a lion (*mundu*) symbolises the bridegroom in marriage initiation rites.

Adaptation is an important component of culture. Adaptation is the process through which human and non-human forms of life cope with environmental forces and stresses by changing in such a way as to fit their habitat. Unlike other forms of life human beings have both biological and cultural means of adaptation. Biological adaptations include genetic adaptation, long-term and short-term physiological adaptation.[25] Cultural adaptation involves devising means of coping with the environment such as the cultivation of suitable sources of food.

Culture is an important aspect of human adaptation. Cultural anthropology examines cultural diversity in the present and recent past while archaeology reconstructs behaviour in the past by analysing material remains.[26] Cultural anthropology, focusing on human culture, identifies, interprets, and explains social and cultural similarities and differences. It engages with two kinds of activities, the one referred to as ethnography and based on field work, and the other called ethnology and focused on cross-cultural comparison.[27] Archaeological anthropology reconstructs and interprets past human behaviour and cultural patterns by studying material remains. Through excavation, archaeologists find artefacts, tools, weapons and rests of buildings from past cultures. They may also collect plant and animal remains and ancient garbage all of which tell stories about consumption and activities in the past.[28]

There are many ways in which cultures can change. One of these is by borrowing traits of other cultures in a process known as diffusion. Cultures are never truly isolated. Contact between neighbouring cultures results in the exchange of values, practices, and ideas. Cultural diffusion may occur through intermarriage, war, trade, etc.[29] Cultural diffusion is affirmed by acculturation or the exchange of cultural features through first hand contact. In the process of acculturation parts of the cultures involved may change, but cultural groups remain distinct from each other. In some cases a mixed language develops between cultures to ease communication. In situations where cultures are in continuous contact with each other, they may exchange and blend foods, music, dances, clothing, and tools.[30]

Another way in which cultural diffusion occurs is through independent invention whereby humans creatively find solutions to problems. Thus, in the course of history, agriculture has been invented. Similarly, economic evolution has resulted in cultural change. In Africa, the HIV and AIDS pandemic has led to changes in cultural practices. Some existing practices, for example, levirate marriage, have been abandoned for fear of contracting the virus.

Contemporary concepts of human rights challenge cultural relativism by promoting values of justice and morality beyond the confines of specific cultures and religions. The Universal Declaration of Human Rights promotes the rights of individuals. In Africa, cultural practices such as female genital mutilation (FGM) have been challenged. FGM takes place in the form of clitoridectomy (the removal of a girl's clitoris) or of infibulation which involves sewing up the lips (labia) of the vagina so as to constrict the vaginal opening. Both procedures limit female sexual pleasure, and therefore, are believed to reduce levels of adultery among women. Human rights activists condemn both procedures as they infringe on the human rights of women.[31] It must be noted that none of the tribes in Zambia practice FGM. However, herbs are used to promote vagina tightening.

Globalisation also fosters cultural diffusion. As a social phenomenon "globalisation encompasses a series of processes, including diffusion and acculturation, working to promote change in a world in which nations and people are increasingly interlinked and mutually dependent."[32] The social media adds to the spreading of cultural values globally. As a result, there is today what could be called a hybridization or mixing of cultures.

In the study of cultures we are faced with the problem of ethnocentrism. Ethnocentrism is the tendency to view one's own culture as superior and to apply its values when judging the behaviour and beliefs of people raised in other cultures. Ethnocentrism contributes to social solidarity and to a sense of shared values and community among people. However, it has disadvantages. Cultural relativism implies that behaviour in one culture should not be judged by the standards of another culture. Cultural relativism argues that there exists no superior culture nor a universal culture or morality. The moral and ethical rules of all cultures deserve equal respect.[33] Being in agreement with this view, the present author does not consider Bemba culture as superior to any other culture. Rather, he analyses marriage and female initiation rites among the Bemba people of Zambia to demonstrate that African cultures embody gendered economic, religious, and political ideologies.

As a way of organising social life, cultures have introduced taboos. Cultural organisation depends on social interactions for its expression and continuation. People are organised in groups or families. For example, in pre-colonial Bemba communities, marriage taboos were introduced for the sake of organising families. Although marriage between cousins was allowed, generally one was not expected to marry a blood sister or first cousin. There was a strong taboo on incest (prohibition of marrying or mating with a close relative). Incest was discouraged and punished in a variety of ways. Exogamy, which is marrying outside one's group, was encouraged. Parents would normally choose a particular family to which they would like to see their child linked through marriage.

2.5 GENDER

Gender refers to socially determined ideas and practices of what it is to be female or male.[34] Gender perceptions are based on cultural constructs of sexual differences.[35] At the same time sex refers to the biological characteristics that categorize someone as female or male. On the basis of biological differences, culture associates gender with certain activities, behaviours, and ideas. Some cultures recognise more than two genders. Many of the behavioural and attitudinal differences between the sexes emerge from culture rather than from biology. While sex differences are biological, gender refers to those traits that a culture assigns to males and females. This means that culture constructs male and female identities and the characteristics expected from each.[36]

Gender roles are the activities a culture assigns to each sex. Related to gender roles are gender stereotypes which are oversimplified but strongly held ideas about male and female behaviour. 'Gender stratification' describes the uneven distribution of resources between men and women. Gender stratification varies from one culture to another, depending on the economical situation, the political system, the rule of descent, and post-marital residence patterns. Socially valued resources include power, prestige, and personal freedom. A particular distribution of labour, whereby women mainly work at home and men do productive labour, may reinforce a perception of men as being more valuable because they are public workers and of women as active in private surroundings and, therefore, less valuable.[37] In pre-colonial Bemba society, for example, different roles were assigned to women and men. Women worked on the farms, collected firewood, fetched water, and brew beer while men were hunters and warriors.

Many African societies promote patriarchy: the rule of fathers, or a political system in which women have an inferior social, political, and religious status, and fewer basic human rights. However, different rules regarding descent and post-marital residence lead to cross-cultural variations in gender status. In societies with a matrilineal descent system and matrilocality, the status of women tends to be high. Matrilocality means that a married couple resides with the wife's relatives. In other words, the husband moves to join the wife's family leading to the dispersion of males rather than consolidating their status as is the case in a patrilineal descent system. Clearly, women have a high status in matrilineal, matrilocal societies where descent group membership, succession to political positions, allocation of land, and overall social identity all involve females.

Women in such a context have considerable influence beyond their households and form the basis of the entire social structure. Although it may still appear as if public authority is assigned to men, much of the power and of the right to make decisions belongs to older women in the community. Anthropologists have insisted that in a matrilineal society there is matriarchy. Women's political and ritual influence usually rivals that of men.[4] Sometimes patriarchy may be deeply entrenched into the fabric of society. Women may be in leadership and ritual positions, but in general practice power still rests in the hands of men.[38] Differences expressed in terms of gender stratification can be reduced by men fulfilling roles that remove them from the local community, for example, when women play prominent roles locally while men pursue activities in a wider, regional context. There also are matrifocal societies that are not necessarily matrilineal. The combination of males travelling and females fulfilling prominent economic roles in their place of permanent residence may result in an improved status of women. A matrifocal society is mother-centered with husbands and/or fathers often working elsewhere. Some matrifocal societies are patrilineal and in that case descent is through the male line.[39]

In traditional Bemba society, men hunted and fished, but women controlled the local economy. Women did some fishing, would occasionally hunt (*ukusowa*) and gather fruit, but their major productive role was farming. Women owned land which they had inherited from matrilineal kinswomen. They controlled the production and distribution of food. A council of male chiefs managed military operations, but chiefly succession was matrilineal. Thus, women controlled alliances between descent groups. Such alliances were in tribal society an important political tool. Patrilineal and patrilocal systems, on the other hand, keep males in a family together and united. Patrilocality means that, after marriage, a couple lives with the husband's kin. Pressure on the resources in a community may result in the decline of a matrilineal system and the spread of patrilineal-patrilocal social structures. The customs of patrilineal-patrilocal indigenous communities often encourage the waging of warfare against other villages as married men continue to live with their kinsmen in their home village where they form strong alliances for doing battle.[40]

Gender ideologies, in general, define rights and responsibilities as well as 'appropriate' behaviour for women and men in society. In many contexts, dominant cultures reinforce the position of those who wield economic, political and social power which usually comes down to the buttressing of male power. In contemporary society, globalization contributes to the diffusion of cultures, particularly western culture.

Thus, today, a community may experience *anomie*, a state of normlessness because traditional norms have been abandoned and no new ones have yet been developed.[41]

Gender ideologies are concerned with the status of women and men in their communities. The status of a person determines how he or she is ranked and treated in society. One acquires a certain status by being born into it or through one's achievements. People also may acquire a different status at certain points in their life cycle.[42] For example, in Bemba society, the status of a young woman or young man changes when they get married and after having a child in which case they are considered as truly adult (*umukulu*), even if they are younger than eighteen. Someone over thirty who is not married is still seen as a youngster (*umwaice*). The status of a person may also be perceived as based on his or her gender, race, and social class. Society tends to categorize people according to their status, thereby, creating a system of social stratification. People with a low status are at the bottom of the social stratification system. Often such persons are stigmatized and face prejudice and discrimination. In most African societies, single mothers, barren women, widows and widowers, albinos and the disabled have a low status. Some persons are associated with a number of statuses called a status set. For example, the child of a king may have the status both of a married person and of a royal (*uwakubufumu*).

Gender and status in society are associated with specific ways of behaving. One is expected to behave as one's status requires and to perform one's role in society in accordance with the social norms associated with one's status. Norms are general rules that guide people's behaviour in society.[43] Social norms help to structure society in a way that is organized and predictable. However, when normative rules become too rigid, stereotypes and prejudices may emerge. Stereotypes are oversimplified and generalized conceptions. In Africa, and in many other parts of the world, the status of males and of females is stereotyped according to the roles they are expected to perform by virtue of being male or female or by virtue of their biological make up. Women are perceived to be weaker than men. Such stereotypes may result in sexism, a belief that women are inferior to men.[44] Lindsey notes that "sexism is perpetuated by systems of patriarchy, male-dominated societal structures leading to the oppression of women. Patriarchy exhibits androcentrism whereby male-centered norms become the standard to which all members of a community adhere.[45]

The categorization of gender and sex also accommodates persons in contemporary society who don't fit in the conservative categories of male and female. There are, for example, people who undergo surgery to make their gender identity consistent with their biological sex or to make their biological sex consistent with their gender identity because they think that they were born in the wrong body. Depending on one's sexual orientation, one may prefer sexual partners of one gender above the other. Some people are born with ambiguous sex characteristics. They may be assigned a particular sex at birth but develop a different sexual identity as they grow up. Some cultures, especially in the global north, allow people to move freely between genders, regardless of their biological sex. Other cultures don't allow such freedom. This means that cultures, or communities, influence their members' choice of sex roles. People often speak of gender roles rather than of sex roles. Gender roles are forged within a sociocultural context.[46]

GENDER CONCEPTS

Culture
Culture refers to distinctive patterns of ideas, beliefs, and norms which characterize the way of life and relations of a society or of a group in a society.

Gender analysis
Gender analysis is a systematic gathering and examination of information on gender differences and social relations to identify, understand, and redress inequities based on gender. Gender discrimination is a systematically unfavorable treatment of individuals on the basis of their gender, denying them their human rights, opportunities, and/or resources.

Gender division of labour
The socially determined ideas and practices which define what roles and activities are deemed appropriate for women and men.

Gender equality and equity
Gender equality denotes women having the same opportunities in life as men, including the ability to participate in the public sphere. Gender equity denotes the equivalence in life outcomes for women and men, recognizing their different needs and interests, and requiring a redistribution of power and resources.

Gender mainstreaming
Gender mainstreaming means to introduce a gender perspective into all aspects of a country's policy and activities by building gender capacity and accountability. This may require gender planning which involves technical and political processes and procedures necessary

to implement gender-sensitive policy. Gender mainstreaming addresses gender relations - hierarchical relations of power between women and men that tend to disadvantage women.

Gender violence
This refers to any act or threat by members of one sex that inflicts physical, sexual, or psychological harm on members of the opposite sex because of their gender.

Patriarchy
Patriarchy is a systemic societal structure that institutionalizes male physical, social, and economic power over women.

Sex and gender
Sex refers to the biological characteristics that categorize someone as either female or male; whereas, gender refers to the socially determined ideas and practices of what it is to be female or male.

Women's empowerment
Women's empowerment refers to a process of transforming gender power relations starting from grassroots level through individuals, groups, organizations, governments, and religions by developing an awareness of women's subordination and building their capacity to challenge it. This awareness contributes to the recognition that women's rights are human rights and that women experience injustices, solely because of their gender.

Gender ideologies
Gender ideologies define rights and responsibilities as well as 'appropriate' behaviour by women and men. These gender ideologies often reinforce male power and the idea of women's inferiority.

Androcentrism

Male-centered norms operating throughout all social institutions that become the standard to which all persons adhere.

Gender expression

Gender expression refers to the way in which a person acts to communicate gender within a given culture, for example, in terms of clothing, communication patterns, and interests. A person's gender expression may or may not be consistent with socially prescribed gender roles and may or may not reflect one's gender identity.

Sexual orientation

Sexual orientation refers to the sex of those to whom one is sexually and romantically attracted. Categories of sexual orientation typically include the attraction to members of one's own sex (gay men or lesbians), attraction to members of the other sex (heterosexuals), and attraction to members of both sexes (bisexuals). While these categories continue to be widely used, research suggests that sexual orientation does not always appear in such definable categories but rather on a continuum. In addition, some research indicates that sexual orientation is fluid for some, possibly especially for women.

Coming out

Coming out refers to the process in which one acknowledges and accepts one's sexual orientation. It encompasses the process in which one discloses one's sexual orientation to others.

Closeted

The term 'closeted' refers to a state of secrecy or cautious privacy regarding one's sexual orientation.

2.6 CONCLUSION

African societies perform initiation rites to mark the transition from one stage of life to another. The rites take a person from a lower to a higher level in society. Sociological, anthropological, cultural, and gender concepts help scholars to understand culture and how social systems define the positions of man and woman in society. Sociology, by definition, is the study of the interaction between institutions such as family and religion and of the manner in which societies get transformed. Anthropology, on the other hand, is the holistic comparative study of humanity, exploring human biological and cultural diversity.

Culture and religion are social constructs. Culture refers to patterns of ideas, beliefs, and norms that characterize a society's way of life and its relations. Religion is a cultural universal, consisting of beliefs and behaviour concerned with transcendent or supernatural forces. Culture and religion construct gender roles in society. Gender roles reflect the socially determined ideas and practices of what it is to be female or male.

CHAPTER THREE

FEMINISM: ORIGINS AND DEVELOPMENT

3.1 INTRODUCTION

The social movement, theory, and political commitment that advocates for giving women the same social, political, and economic rights as men is known as feminism. The history of feminism can be traced back to the French Revolution at the end of the 18th century and to the 19th century industrial revolution in England and elsewhere in western Europe when women awoke to the realization that, even though they fully participated in industrial labour, their social, political, and economic status remained well below that of their male counterparts. Feminism uses the experience of women as the starting point for social, political, and religious analyses. Rosemary Radford Reuther notes:

> Human experience is the starting point and the ending point of the hermeneutical circle. Codified tradition both reaches back to roots in experience and is constantly renewed or discarded through the test of experience. 'Experience' includes experience of the

divine, experience of oneself, and experience of the community and world, in an interacting dialectic.[1]

It has been observed that almost everywhere in the world women have a lower social status than men. They are discriminated in social, economic, political, and religious contexts. The relationship between race, class, and gender and the distribution of power and resources are both controlled by male elite. As a result, contemporary global society is patriarchal and male-dominated. Within feminism there are different ideological positions such as liberal, radical, and Marxist or socialist.[2]

3.2 HISTORICAL DEVELOPMENT

According to Susan Rakoczy, Hubertine Auclert was the first woman to use the word 'feminism' in 1882, referring to the struggle of women in Europe and North America for political rights.[3] Three waves are distinguished in the development of feminism based on different political emphases.

The first wave in the 19th and early 20th centuries focused on obtaining political rights among these the right to vote. First-wave feminists contributed to the abolition of slavery, to prison reforms, better conditions for the mentally ill, and the improvement of education. The movement advocated for recognition of the dignity of slaves brought from Africa to the Americas and freedom of women who were marginalised in patriarchal societies. It was based on the appreciation of the full humanity of women, and it aimed to reconstruct society so that it would reflect the equality of women and men.[4] Rakoczy notes:

The focus of this first wave of feminism was women's

suffrage. In Britain and North America, women demonstrated publicly, fasted, chained themselves to the fences surrounding government buildings were arrested and imprisoned. They were derided as crazy fanatics, the antithesis of what "good" women should be. Gradually the right to vote was recognised in various Western countries, beginning with New Zealand in 1893. The contributions of women to the war effort during World War 1 (1914-1918) paved the way for the vote to be speedily given to women. Now it is an accepted right in nearly all countries.[5]

First-wave feminism ended when the right to vote was won in the early 1920s. The challenges of the economic depression in the 1930s and the Second World War in the 1940s gave towards the 1960s rise to a second wave of feminism. This new feminism was also shaped by the civil rights movement for political and social equality of black people in the western world.[6] Second-wave feminism gathered momentum in the 1950s and 1960s in the United States. Women, increasingly aware of the need for freedom, demonstrated for equal pay for equal work, reproductive rights such as contraception and abortion, and for the legal recognition of their human dignity. The movement also exerted pressure on religious institutions to accept women as members of the clergy.[7]

Third-wave feminism took off towards the end of the 1970s and continues into the present. Until the 1970s, the experience of western white, middle-class women was taken to be the standard and norm for all women in the world. Realising their differences, African-American and Hispanic women in the United States began to challenge the dominance of white women in second-wave feminism and made the point that not all women experience injustice only because they happen to be female. Women in different parts of the world have different experiences of oppression. The oppression of African women, for example, takes on different forms from that experienced by white women in the west, surely not just middle-class women. Thus, third-wave feminism includes the voices of African, Asian, and Latin-American women, including women belonging to indigenous cultures. Their oppression, they argue, is based on race and economic status intertwined with sexism.[8]

Sexism results from male power and prejudice under-girded by dominant patriarchal structures in society. When prejudice goes together with power, it can grow into an ideology characterised by a sense of superiority and resulting in sexism, racism, anti-Semitism, or other manifestations of prejudice. Such ideologies can be traced back to the thought of the Greek philosopher Aristotle (384-322 BCE) who described society as a series of hierarchical relations.[9] According to Aristotle and Greek dualism, it is natural and normal for one who is superior to govern those who are inferior. Women are, therefore, to be governed by men at all times. Thus, Greek philosophy has reinforced patriarchy and the marginalisation of women. Patriarchy is at the root of sexism and many other 'isms' including racism, colonialism, and economic classism.[10]

Different terms are used to refer to feminist theory and feminist political commitment because in some parts of the world the term feminism is associated with fundamentalist women who dislike men. In many parts of Africa, including Zambia, feminism is associated with women who are 'uncultured,' not married, or who don't respect their husbands. Such views are the result of a lack of information about the origin and development of feminism. In addition, the first non-governmental organisation to advocate for gender equality in Africa was western funded and condemned cultural values that form the basis of African marriage. Thus, gender issues and feminism came to be seen as a preoccupation of unmarried women who had forsaken African cultural values. As a result women who were married and loyal to established African social institutions distanced themselves from the movement.

Many African-American women in the United States use the term 'womanist' to describe themselves. The word was first used by Alice Walker who stated that womanists advocate for the survival and wholeness of people, both male and female. Women of colour in America prefer the term 'womanist' because they feel that 'feminism' meets only the needs of white women who focus on gender issues. They insist that black women have different experiences of oppression because, generally, men of all races are, with the participation of white women, involved in marginalising black women.[11] Sarojini Nadar, a South African of Indian origin, also prefers to use the term 'womanist' as opposed to feminist.[12] She agrees that 'feminist' does not adequately represent the experience of non-white South Africans. Some Hispanic women use the word *mujerista* to indicate their views on the oppression of women originating from Central and South American countries but living in North America. It is clear from the above that there is a good deal of diversity in feminism worldwide today.

Feminism follows constructive as well as deconstructive methods. It uses the 'See, judge, and act' hermeneutics. It is deconstructive in that it adopts a critical stance, asking questions and not taking the past for granted. It applies reflection as an intrinsic tool in inquiry. Feminism reconstructs through praxis, referring to a transformative action. It is, in other words, an engaged action leading to change and responding to the diversity of women's experiences globally.[13] Women's experiences of a cultural nature in their own specific racial and ethnic situations, of poverty or wealth, of political ideologies and religious doctrines, give rise to different political commitments.

3.3 BRANCHES OF FEMINISM

Feminist theory takes account of the diversity of women's experience in society. Hence, there are several branches of feminism, each with its own concerns. On the basis of women's experiences and perceptions, feminism challenges oppression and discrimination and advances "political goals that offer gender equality."[14]

3.3.1 Liberal feminism

Liberal feminism views people as created equal. No one should be denied opportunities because of his or her gender. Liberal feminism is also called egalitarian or mainstream feminism. It insists that women must enjoy the same rights as men because people are born equal whatever their gender, race, class, and colour. Liberal feminists argue that both genders benefit if sexism, racism, classism, and patriarchy are eliminated from society. They do not believe in a complete restructuring of society to achieve empowerment and equitable societal roles for women. Liberal feminism draws on Enlightenment notions, and it sees equal access for men and women to education and personal rights as a rational requirement. It is the most moderate type of feminism, and it is advocated by women who have no issues with the overall structure of the contemporary social system except that they wish it to be nonsexist.[15]

Some liberal feminists embrace cultural feminism that seeks to emphasise the positive qualities associated with women's roles such as nurturing, caring, cooperation, and mutual connection.[16]

3.3.2 Socialist or Marxist feminism

Socialist or Marxist feminism employs a model based on the views of Marx and Engels who associated the inferior position of women in society with class-based capitalism and its promotion of the patriarchal family in modern societies.[17] The argument goes that capitalism, patriarchy, sexism, classism, and racism are interwoven. The unpaid domestic labour of women in many societies serves patriarchy and capitalism.[18] Economic and emotional dependency go together. In a country like Zambia where male agency is the norm, a man's loss of economic status implies a loss of ideal masculinity and results in emotional problems. This leads men to preserve a patriarchal stance to protect their economic privileges.

Marxist or socialist feminists argue that women did not always occupy inferior positions in pre-modern societies. In primitive societies, women were equal and even superior to men. Some women were cultural leaders because food gathering was more important for survival than hunting. Marxist feminists see family as an institution that has contributed to the marginalisation of women in society. In their view, the family did not develop to fulfill human needs for companionship because these were catered for by the communal clan. Rather, its focus has been the preservation of wealth within the paternal line, and as a result, women have been turned into breeders of sons who continue the family line and inherit the family property.[19]

Socialist feminism appeals to working-class women and to those who feel disadvantaged by the capitalist economic system. Among these are women who have double responsibilities, doing domestic duties without payment and working in the labour force as well. The only difference between classic Marxist theory and socialist feminist theory is that the former focuses on property and economic conditions while the latter includes issues around sexism and gender.[20] The theory is limited in that it focuses on working-class women when, in fact, not all women get the opportunity to work.

3.3.3 Radical feminism

Radical feminism is fully focused on the oppression of women by their male counterparts. It is an ideological movement that attributes women's inferior standing in society to a class system based on patriarchy and dividing the sexes. In the nineteenth century, women in America who were active in the anti-slavery movement began to identify oppressive tendencies of male colleagues. The same observations were made during the second wave of feminism in the twentieth century.[21] As Lindsey notes, radical feminism holds that "sexism is at the core of patriarchal society and that all social institutions reflect sexism." Unlike liberal feminism which is concerned with the workplace and legal changes, radical feminism focuses on the patriarchal family as the main arena where domination and oppression take place.[22] Because it is women who become pregnant and bear children, it is assumed that they are the natural nurturers. Their role in the reproduction process has led to a division of labour whereby women's responsibilities tend to keep them at home in a serving, subordinate position. Radical feminists are convinced that women's oppression stems from male domination. They reason that, if the problem is not men, capitalism nor socialism or any other male-dominated system will provide a solution. Therefore, women have to create separate institutions that are women-centered and that rely on women rather than men.[23] They advocate for technology and for contraceptives to relieve women from the burden of pregnancy especially when they are not ready for it. Radical feminists are in favour of abortion if pregnancy is the result of rape or incest or if the unborn baby puts the health of the mother at risk.[24]

3.3.4 Multicultural feminism

Multicultural feminism is concerned with the marginalization of women by social and multicultural conditions. It focuses, for example, on how colonization, race, class, and the oppression of women in the global south are interrelated. It considers cultural elements and historical conditions that foster the oppression of women, including occurrences where women are subjected to certain forms of punishment for the simple reason that they are women.[25] The theory opposes the restriction of women's rights such as denying girls education for reasons of culture or religion.

3.3.5 Global feminism

Global feminism holds that no woman is free until the conditions that oppress women worldwide are eliminated. Good quality health care, education, and paid employment are crucial for the emancipation of women globally.[26] Like cultural feminism, global feminist theory opposes the restriction of women's rights on the basis of cultural or religious considerations.[27]

3.3.6 Ecofeminism

Ecofeminism is a new branch of feminism. It sees the oppression and marginalization of women as associated with the exploitation of the planet earth. Ecofeminism draws on earth-based spiritual imagery, arguing that world religions such as Christianity and Islam have an ethical responsibility to challenge a patriarchal system that exploits the planet and discriminates women. Earth can be healed and ecological balance restored through political action that emphasizes the equality of all species.[28] Ecofeminism is related to claims made by environmentalists and animal activists, but it extends its concerns to include the well-being of the entire ecosystem. Ecofeminists argue that "protecting an animal or a plant because it is a member of an endangered species is still a highly individualistic idea."[29] They insist that "Species are not endangered in isolation, but because the ecosystems of forest, prairie, or wetland in which they live are endangered."[30] In their view, the current ecological crisis can be brought to an end by emphasizing the equality of all species, human and non-human, as well as earth-mysteries.

3.4 GENDER ROLES AND CONCEPTUAL FRAMEWORKS

In this section, different conceptual and theoretical frameworks are used to explain gender roles and clarify related empirical aspects of gender inequality in the light of feminism and feminist political commitment.

3.4.1 Structural functionalism

Structural functionalism is a macro-sociological[31] theory based on the premise that society is made up of interdependent parts each of which contributes to the functioning of society as a whole. It holds that social control and stability are fostered when members of a community have beliefs and values in common.[32]

Structural functionalists suggest that in pre-modern societies, such as that of the Bemba people before the introduction of Christianity and colonialism, social equilibrium was achieved by assigning different tasks to men and women. Men served as hunters and fishermen while women worked as farmers and housekeepers. Some communities in modern society apply the same principles by assigning complementarity and mutuality in gender roles. In other words, social order is maintained through value consensus. The trouble with this theory is that conservatives have used it as justification for male dominance. It implies that women can, apart from fulfilling their domestic tasks, only serve as supplementary or reserve labour for men.[33]

3.4.2 Social conflict theory

The social conflict theory is based on the view that social control and stability are achieved involuntarily through the power exercised by one social class over another. Drawing on Karl Marx, the conflict theory presents society as a stage on which struggles for power over resources take place. It involves a capitalistic mentality whereby power is consolidated in the hands of a few members of the ruling class (*bourgeoisie*). The theory assumes that only when the oppressed recognize their common oppression and develop a class consciousness, can they unite and obtain the necessary resources to seriously challenge the status quo. Friedrich Engels, Marx's collaborator, applied these same principles to family units and gender roles. According to him, a household is an autocracy where the supremacy of the husband should not be questioned.[34] In contemporary society, the conflict theory has been redefined to make it more palatable for people who pursue social change leading to egalitarianism. However, the principle of society as a battlefield for power and resources where men are privileged and women disadvantaged remains valid. Lindsey notes:

> Conflict theory focuses on the social placement function of the family that deposits people at birth into families who possess varying degrees of economic resources. People fortunate enough to be deposited into wealthier families will work to preserve existing inequality and the power relations in the broader

society because they clearly benefit from the overall power of balance. Social class *endogamy* (marrying within the same class) and inheritance patterns ensure that property and wealth are kept in the hands of a few powerful families.[35]

In this way, power imbalances and domination are institutionalized, and oppression becomes accepted and legitimated by the privileged as well as the oppressed. The notion that a family is deservedly wealthy and that those born into poor families stay poor because they lack talent and a good work ethic is thus perpetuated.[36]

A weak point of this theory is that it overemphasizes the economic basis of inequality and the assumption that there will always be competition between husband and wife or between family members. Men are portrayed as being consciously out to oppress women and little attention is given to other factors that may lead to the oppression of women. The theory denies women any opportunity for expanding their economic activities and attain equality with men. Men, on the other hand, are also denied the chance to develop their domestic talents and to fulfill nurturing roles like women.[37]

3.4.3 Symbolic interaction theory

The symbolic interaction theory explains social interaction as a dynamic process whereby people, in response to interaction, continually modify their behavior. Society and its institutions exist only through human interaction. As Lindsey notes in her concept of 'end point fallacy': "The negotiation of social reality is an ongoing process in which new definitions produce new behavior in a never-ending cycle."[38] The 'end point fallacy' is the reason people change their behavior when they move from one context to another.

Symbolic interaction theory sees reality as a social construct. Social interaction is controlled by norms that are determined by culture. These norms offer general guidelines for role behavior. Human beings have latitude in how they act out their roles. In other words, the context of interaction is a key determinant of role performance. According to symbolic interaction theory, concepts such as race, ethnicity, and gender which society uses to categorize people, emerge through a socially constructed process. Thus, the notions of male and female involve certain traits defined as feminine or masculine. Gender labels promote a pattern of competition, rejection, or segregation between the sexes. The construction of the genders as different advantages men who have more power which they use to justify the perceived inequality of those with less power.[39]

The weakness of this theory lies in its focusing on micro-level rather than macro-level processes. In other words, it pays no attention to macro-level processes that may limit people's choice of action, prompting them to engage in gendered behavior opposed to what they would prefer to do. "In some cultures, for example, women and men are dictated by both law and custom to engage in certain occupations, enter into marriages with people they would not choose on their own, and be restricted from attending school."[40] Furthermore, men and women interact according to the roles they play in society. If a man is a social or political leader, his role in society may shape the way he behaves at home. In other words, "power and privilege can result in a patriarchal family regardless of the couple's desire for a more egalitarian arrangement."[41]

3.4.4 Feminist sociological theory
Feminist sociological theory seeks to challenge the biases and prejudices in society that are disadvantageous to women. It uncovers the andro-

centric bias in society. Feminist sociological theory is similar to conflict theory as it holds that "structured social inequality is maintained by ideologies that are frequently accepted by both the privileged and the oppressed."[42] These ideologies become blurred only when oppressed groups gain the resources necessary to do so. Conflict theory focuses on issues of social class and on economic concerns prevailing in society on individual (micro-) levels as well as on institutional (macro-) levels. Feminist theory, however, concentrates on the oppression of women and defines ways in which women can exert control over their destinies and access resources. The oppression of women is based on their gender, class, and race. However, women possess agency: the power to adapt, or alternately, to effect change in difficult circumstances.[43]

By and large the western concept of feminism should be credited for exposing how the patriarchal status quo and andro-centrism pervade theories and ideologies. It has clarified how the interlocking of sexism, classism, and racism serves to perpetuate patriarchy and the marginalization of women. Nonetheless, African women and their male allies have observed that there is need to redefine feminism and gender in ways that speak to the African worldview.

3.5 TOWARDS AN AFRICAN CONCEPT OF FEMINISM AND GENDER

The media has reinforced gender and feminist stereotypes. Its dissemination of information tends to foster misogynism, and it often presents gender questions and feminism as the concerns of women who are frustrated and do not like men. Lindsey rightly notes:

> In addition to highlighting disagreement among feminists, media depict feminists as puritanical, man-

hating, lesbian or butch, taking unfair advantage of men in the workplace and controlling men in their homes...Jokes deriding feminism about their appearance, sexuality and love life, and how they control their children and husbands are common.[44]

Men who sympathize with feminism face enmity and are considered as lacking the values of ideal masculinity. Women who advocate for the rights of their gender are labeled as outspoken and uncultured.[45] In Africa, the misogynistic portrayal of feminism has been fostered by the commercialization of gender concerns. Many individuals and NGOs have come up with projects that purport to promote gender equality but that are driven by purely commercial interests. Given the different experiences of women, it would appear that current approaches to feminist politics emphasize gender rather than feminism as such. Gender is inclusive and involves the striving for equal rights of, and opportunities for, men and women. Feminists in Africa have begun to (re)define the oppression of women in their own terms. Many guilds of women are attempting to chart ways in which African women can realise freedom and dignity. One such guild is the Circle of Concerned African Women Theologians.

It is becoming increasingly clear in the African context that patriarchy may not mean the same thing as in the western world. Western feminism has been criticized for assuming that patriarchy is a homogeneous phenomenon. By emphasizing the oppression of women in marriage and family life, feminism tends to minimize the practical benefits of marriage. It has been observed that, seen through western lenses, an African marriage may look like a patriarchal arrangement. However, their marriage setup may offer African women not only a social support system but also such important economic resources that their concerns about subordination pale in comparison.[46]

Research has shown that women in traditional marriages are as satisfied with their choices as women in egalitarian marriages. In his study of notions of patriarchy and masculinity in Lusaka, Zambia, Adrian van Klinken concludes that women are more concerned with having a husband who is caring and who provides for their daily needs than with issues of male headship.[47] According to Van Klinken, Zambian women have no problem with male headship provided that the man is responsible and fulfills his duties as head of the family. He argues that the monolithic understanding of patriarchy that is current in traditional feminism hinders a more perceptive interpretation. Patriarchy in some African communities, for example, in Zambia, does not necessarily mean male dominance. Rather, it refers to male agency.[48] In addition, putting too much emphasis on human agency may distract us from those cases in which women are indeed victimized and ignored by law.[49] In all this, what comes to the fore is that, in relation to Africa, patriarchy and feminism should be defined on the basis of African women's experiences. Western answers may not adequately answer African questions, and vice versa.

3.6 CONCLUSION

The political theory of radical feminism is premised on the conviction that male supremacy and oppression are the defining characteristics of contemporary society. All feminist ideologies agree that women as compared to men live oppressed lives and are under-represented in all sectors of society. Feminists differ in their explanations of the causes of inequality and in their strategies for eliminating patriarchy in society. These differences are among the reasons Africans should interpret feminism using African thought and experiences.

CHAPTER FOUR

RITUAL, POWER, AND IDEOLOGIES

4. 1 INTRODUCTION

Rituals make the audacious claim that human beings personally, bodily, culturally, and communally can participate in the supernatural by means of ceremonies that imbue the ordinary with a sense of the supernatural. In rituals, the outward and visible convey that which is inward and spiritual. They show that human beings and their ancestors, the supernatural and the earth-mysteries, exist communally. Rituals are mediators of power and ideologies. Chapter four highlights the place of ritual in relationships of power. Rodney Werline rightly observes that "power does not simply exist as an ideal, but in the ability of humans to influence the actions of other humans."[1]

4.2 INITIATION CEREMONIES AS RITES OF PASSAGE

Marriage and female Chisungu initiation rites in Bemba society are part of the rites of passage. Arnold van Gennep analyses the fundamental processes underlying the change of an individual's status in society. Life is characterised by transitions from one social group or situation to another. Individuals pass through different age grades, social relationships, and occupations.[2] Willet and Deegan note:

> Rites of passage are subdivided into three stages: separation (preliminal), transition (liminal), and incorporation (post-liminal). Rites of separation symbolically detach the individual from an existing point in the social structure. After this separation, the former social status no longer applies to the individual. In the transition or liminal stage, the individual is a symbolic outsider with no clearly derived status or role.[3]

During the rites of passage the liminal person (the "liminar") resides at the margins of society while he or she prepares to adopt a new role in life. The final stage of the ritual sees the individual in his or her new status re-entering society. If this re-entry does not occur, the liminal state continues.[4]

Victor Turner observes that society is a "structure of positions" and the liminal stage marks the transition between two socially viable positions.[5] The initiates or liminars are moving between fixed points. They "are betwixt between the positions assigned and arrayed by law, custom, convention and ceremonial."[6]

There is ambiguity and paradox in the social situation of liminal persons. They are no longer children and not yet adults. As a result, the initiate or the liminal person is often invisible, both structurally and physically. Structural invisibility is the result of being without a social status, and members of society find it difficult to interact with liminars because they fall outside social categories and in a sense they are non-persons.[7]

The taboos that apply to liminars limit their social interaction and foster their social invisibility. Among the Bemba people of Zambia, liminality is accompanied by the seclusion of the initiates.

During marriage and Chisungu female initiation rites, initiates take on an androgynous quality. The initiate may be assigned characteristics of both genders, of the opposite gender, or be treated as genderless. Different sacred emblems (*imbusa*) give expression to the state of liminality. During marriage initiation rites, there is a stage when the bride and bridegroom are taught together and they dress alike and behave similarly. Also sexual activity is affected. Sometimes abstinence is stressed, but a greater degree of sexual freedom may also be allowed. In other words, in the liminal stage of rites, sex is treated as having malleable characteristics.[8]

The liminal stage is symbolically related to death and decomposition. Because he or she is without a position in the social system, it is difficult to classify an initiate as alive or dead. As a result, initiates may be treated as corpses and even be buried. During Chisungu initiation the initiate lives in seclusion and poses a danger to the community due to menstrual blood.[9] Persons who come into contact with the initiate may be contaminated unless they have been 'inoculated' by having undergone the same ritual transformation. As Turner notes, these components of liminality force the initiate to submit to the will of the entire community.[10] During the initiation, the former status of the initiate is erased, creating a blank slate upon which expectations for the new status are imprinted. The initiate is expected to be submissive and humble to the society's values, norms, and relationships.

In Bemba society, initiates in seclusion used to treat each other as equals despite any hierarchical differences that existed prior to the transition. They formed a *communitas.* The relationships formed during *communitas* often would extend beyond the liminal stage; however, liminality in contemporary society is no longer a clearly delineated situation. The difference between the various stages has become blurred and confusing. The lack of clear cohorts, symbols, rituals, and a diminished awareness of the sacred is characteristic for the influence of western worldviews.

4.3 RELIGIO-POLITICAL AND IDEOLOGICAL POWERS OF RITUAL

According to scholarly literature, ritual reflects the relationships between people as they negotiate, mediate, and enact power.[11] A review of African marriage and female initiation rites casts new light on the role of ritual in the micro-politics of everyday life and reveals the way in which tutors of cultural initiation rites attempt to relate their instruction to the larger story of the particular African tribe they belong to. Initiation rites are powerful because they are enacted within a web of political relationships, whether local, national, or international. While not denying or playing down claims by participants that initiation rites are a valuable, significant experience, it is of importance to analyze the way in which such rituals become a factor in politics and in power relationships.

Bemba marriage and female initiation rites include a physical inspection focusing on virginity, labia elongation, vaginal tightening, pregnancy, and male prowess. Those who do not meet the required social norms find themselves stuck in a state of liminality which may sometimes be permanent. For example, barren women, impotent men, and unmarried women who have lost their virginity may be considered as liminars and as such be permanently marginalized and often mocked by society.

They have failed to be incorporated in society. In traditional Bemba society, therefore, people who do not meet the accepted norms—be they barren women, single female non-virgins, or impotent men—remain in the potentially unending liminal stage of a symbolic rite of passage. The community often prevents the reincorporation of people who live in the margins of society because it has no alternative, socially respectable roles to offer them.[12] This makes African groups into marginalizing communities where the opportunities of individuals are limited by subjecting them to a wide range of social restrictions. Nonetheless, marriage and female initiation rites can also serve as a road towards the removal of social restrictions.

Cultures develop ideas about power. And power becomes a reality when one human being is able to impact another human being and to influence his or her actions. In other words, power is relational. Werline notes:

> The understanding of power becomes as complex as the analysis of all the possible ways in which humans relate to one another. A brutal dictator may physically force a people to do his will, but two lovers will structure their days because of the desire to see one another. The dictator controls a people in order to satisfy his maniacal, sociopathic obsessions, while the lovers seek the happiness of the other, but in turn influence one another's action. This comparison of extremes suggests that power is neither necessarily good nor evil. Power can be abusive and destructive – even violent – or it can result in something beautiful and life giving. While it would be wrong to reduce every aspect of every relationship to issues of power, to dismiss power as a

feature of relationship would be just as incorrect.[13]

Anthropologists and sociologists recognize the way in which ritual activity, for example, marriage and initiation rites, enacts relationships between individuals and groups. A ritual can be defined as "a collection of culturally determined behaviours through which humans bodily participate in what is 'really real' to them and enact relationships with one another."[14] Some initiation rites adhere to a fixed use of language and actions, and their ritual practice takes place in appropriate places at specified performance times. However, even if culture does not strictly regulate the various aspects of some initiation rites, performances of all rites display constant patterns. A person need not always speak and act in prescribed ways for his or her action to be ritualised.

How are African marriage and female initiation rites involved in relationships of power? First, marriage and female initiation rites represent embodied actions that mirror the effect of culture on an individual's body. Cultural norms and taboos serve to engrain behaviours.[15] Indeed, controlled behaviours reflect the basic dispositions of human beings and their approach to life's many demands and actions. Recent anthropological and sociological scholarship also shows that power does not simply descend from the top down. Instead, power is manifested in people's daily activities throughout the entire culture in which they function. Nathan Mitchell notes:

> [P]ower is contingent, local, imprecise, national, and organisational...[P]ower is distributed all over the social body; it is a matter of techniques and discursive practices that comprise the micropolitics of everyday life.[16]

African initiation rites are techniques used to navigate and negotiate relationships; thus, rituals do not just mask power and serve as methods of control. Rituals also do not simply constitute symbolic actions. Rather, ritual is power.[17] Bell notes:

> [R]itual does not disguise the exercise of power, nor does it refer, express, or symbolise anything outside itself. In other words, rituals do not refer to politics...they are politics. Ritual is a thing itself. It is power; it acts and it actuates.[18]

African marriage and initiation rites include embodied, non-discursive elements. They also contain speech or discourse. The language of rituals contains and conveys a worldview. It expresses this worldview as natural and given. Combined with practice, the discourse becomes embodied and lived by participants. Language assists in tying rituals to the very fabric of daily life, society, and history. For the participants it can transform any moment into an evocation of participation in, and an encounter with, the ancestors and the spiritual world.

Africans pay particular attention to rituals and power because these may have significant consequences. The consequences range from the potential abuse of power to possibly missing out on a way to manage suffering and to empower the vulnerable members of the community. Marriage and female initiation rites among the Bemba people of Zambia bestow the power of fecundity upon the initiates. The initiates are received in the realm of adulthood and they also became a means to negotiate and navigate power relations between people at the micro-political level. Anthropologists have noticed that humans tend to create rituals to assist in transitional moments. Such transitions are accompanied by a sort of cultural anxiety. Drawing on Arnold van

Gennep's perception of ritual, Victor Turner's research and his concepts of liminality and *communitas* provide a useful theoretical basis for understanding marriage and female initiation rites. [19] Initiation rites represent a liminal moment, a threshold moment. Considered in that light, initiation rites make the 'crossing' take place so that when the initiates graduate, *communitas* can be established and preserved.[20]

Pierre Bourdieu, basing himself on Turner's interpretation, emphasizes that rites of passage mark a distinction between those inside the group and those left outside (*Chitongo munshicindilwa*).[21] Applied to marriage and female initiation rites, the ritual action brings the initiate into the group of the initiated (*Abakulu*), simultaneously assigning a place to the individual within the community's power structure. Participants show deference and respect. The ritual concerned with fertility and well-being in life dominates the discourse and permits the participants to evoke the ancestors and God asking for blessings. This implies that the entire ceremony is acted out in the presence of a higher power (*Mwine conde*) who transforms the meeting of initiates and the period of their seclusion into a numinous moment.

With the initiates living in seclusion and in a state of liminality, the community has lost its normal equilibrium and, hence, its social structures are vulnerable to disturbance. Women use this situation to unite in resistance to patriarchy. In that way, in the midsts of their existence as society's outsiders or liminars, they strengthen communitas, their common bond. Marriage and female initiation rites are performed in a wide range of human relationships, social settings, and individual or historical circumstances. Rituals in African societies may function as part of family dynamics, as expressions of love and concern among friends, or as a way in which the community formalises approval or disapproval of its members' actions.

Rituals may confirm the way in which leadership ties a place and a people to an ideal history, or reflect resistance to patriarchy or otherwise oppressive rule. Ritual sometimes deals with the accusation of one who is innocent and who complains and suffers. As an enactment of the power relationships in a society ritual offers as much variety as there are relationships. Human agents in Bemba culture (and this is true for many other cultures as well) seem possessed of a limitless ingenuity when it comes to adapting ritual to new settings and unique needs. Bemba tutors of initiates (*bana chimbusa*) are particularly adept at using marriage and female initiation rites and the history of Bemba people, applying them to people's lived experience and the micro-politics of everyday life. The social function of ritual lies in their creation of temporary or permanent solidarity among people by strengthening the community.

In African communities, rituals are related to totemism. Totems play an important role and can be animals, plants, or geographical features. In each tribe, groups of people have particular totems. The members of each totemic group believe themselves to be descendants of their totem. Traditionally, they neither kill nor eat a totemic animal. Totemism uses nature as a model for society. The totems are mostly animals and plants that are part of nature. People relate to nature through their totemic association with natural species. Diversity in the natural order is a model for diversity in the social order. The unity of the human social order is enhanced by symbolic association with, and imitation of, the natural order.[22]

In the wake of these perceptions, marriage and female initiation rites and their relation to politics and power in African communities need to be considered anew and new perspectives developed. As power flows through a culture, in part through ritual activity, the various power levels all involve each other. Power is not essentially good or evil. Instead, the focus should be on whether power, at any level of a culture, seeks to give life or to destroy it. In the same context, the roles of marriage and female initiation rites need to be considered. Do these give life or destroy it? It means that discussions concerning marriage and female initiation rites among the Bemba people of Zambia have to take ethical considerations into account as well as the benefits enjoyed by participants in the rites.

4.4 CONCLUSION

Rituals celebrated in African communities are formal and political in nature. They consist in stylized, repetitive, and stereotyped activities performed in special (sacred) places at set times. Rituals include sequences of words and actions invented prior to their current performances.[23] They serve the social function of creating temporary or permanent solidarity among people by promoting an awareness of social community. Totems, sacred emblems symbolising a common identity, play an important role in ritual.[24] The sacred emblems (imbusa) commemorate and tell visual stories about sexuality, gender, masculinity, femininity, motherhood, ancestors, and animals. Women use ritual to preserve the social oneness that the emblems symbolise but at the same time to protest against patriarchy.

CHAPTER FIVE

FUNCTION, FORM, AND PRACTICES OF CHISUNGU INITIATION RITES

5. 1 INTRODUCTION

Initiation rites are an important feature of almost all African societies although they are nowadays performed in shortened versions. All initiation rites carry a responsibility to guide young people from childhood to adulthood.[1] They are rites of transition and take a person from a lower to a higher level in society. Between the two levels is the 'camp', or the liminal phase, during which the initiates live in seclusion and are initiated into the mysteries of life. La Fontaine describes initiation rites as events with a social meaning and symbolic actions.[2] Through initiation rites, the positions of power and social relations within society are clarified. The Bemba people of Zambia perform the Chisungu initiation ceremony in which the ritual process definitely and dramatically creates a period of liminality separating childhood and adulthood.[3] In the following section the function, form, and practices of Chisungu initiation rites are discussed.

5.2 PURPOSE

Chisungu initiation serves four purposes. The first is to mark the transition of the initiate from childhood to adulthood (*Ukumukusha*). The initiate is secluded and not allowed to wash or shave. The seclusion emphasises that the new life will not be without difficulties, and, therefore, the initiate has to pass certain tests of maturity. She is taught about safe sexual intercourse and safe delivery of children.[4] During the rites the lighting of a fire or a candle by her paternal aunt symbolises the nascent fertility of the initiate who is painted with a white powder that symbolically removes the danger of menstrual blood which is represented by red marriage emblems.

The initiate is believed to go through the transition from a calm but unproductive childhood to a potentially dangerous but fertile womanhood. The perception that people in transitional states are exposed to danger is derived from the view that life is sacred. It is believed that that which is sacred also poses dangers and must be dealt with ritually.[5] As life is sacred, menstruation blood is believed to be dangerous.

A second purpose of Chisungu initiation rites is to provide the initiate with lessons (*ukufunda*) about her marital, religious, and social roles in life. While instruction regarding sex and motherhood dominates the tuition, the initiate is also prepared for her religious and social duties.[6] Lessons are conveyed by sacred emblems and songs performed during the rites. In pre-colonial times girls became engaged before reaching puberty. Lessons received during Chisungu initiation included a preparation for married life.

During Chisungu initiation rites the concepts of male and female were constructed and justified by reference to the accepted norms in Bemba society. La Fontaine observes that female initiation rites confirmed the power and authority of women[7] who reacted to the dominating role of men by mocking them. In Bemba society, the image of the masterful husband and his submissive wife is reversed during the Chisungu initiation rites. An opposite portrayal is given of the social positions of men and women. This confirms the ambivalence of a matrilineal society in which males dominate but the descent line goes through women.[8]

Oduyoye argues that, while a matrilineal system may suggest the structural dominance of women, no real power is wielded by women.[9] Even in a matrilineal[10] society ideas associated with masculinity are seen as superior to those related to femininity.

A third aim of the Chisungu initiation rites is to mark the change of status and give the initiate a new identity.[11] The initiate graduates possessing knowledge concerning marital behaviour and social etiquette. She has learned what is expected of a mature Bemba woman. As an initiated woman she assumes a position in the hierarchy of women in society. She is well informed because what is normally taboo, that is, talking about sexuality, has been freely discussed during initiation. Hence, Chisungu is an important resource for sex education.

Finally, initiation rituals aim to provide entertainment. The rites are punctuated by dancing and drinking beer. They offer a distraction from monotonous daily life and an occasion to display social status. At the end of the ceremony initiates get presents.[12]

Simon Kapwepwe notes that in pre-colonial Bemba society initiates were given tuition of various kinds to prepare them for adulthood.[13]

They were secluded for periods of three to six months. If resources were available, the rites would continue for six months. Topics covered included:

- Games and exercises that made initiates strong (*ukuipekanya muli buna chifyashi*). The idea was to give women the strength to cope with the delivery of their children. It was not common for women to experience difficulties in delivering. Safe delivery in case of complications was further ensured by the availability of herbs.
- Farming, harvesting, and storing food. Initiates were taught to be industrious and economical. They learned how to store food and build up reserves (*mumatala*) in case of food shortages. A well organized family always had food and kept some stored away for emergencies (*ukukanaba namulya pungunyu*). Some of the lessons given to initiates would today be grouped under the heading 'home economics'.
- Initiates learned to cook appropriate dishes for different occasions.
- Initiates were told to look well after their future husbands and to be equally caring for his and for their own relatives. The offering of sufficient good food to children, relatives, and visitors was emphasized as a central concern because a selfish person was regarded as a witch.
- Another lesson involved the advice not to be jealous of their husbands without good reason (*ubufuba bwabupuba*). While a woman was breastfeeding it was acceptable for her husband to have sex with her younger sister or cousin so that he would not think of committing adultery with a stranger. This practice was also followed to stop the husband from pressuring his wife for sex as long as they had a young baby. It prevented the

arrival of another child before the baby had been weaned, and it functioned as a form of birth control. It was a traditional way of spacing the arrival of children.

- Initiates were taught to be brave when attacked by enemies. Women were not expected to run away and leave their husbands and children in the hands of enemies.
- It was important to be hard working and strong in all aspects of life.
- Among the requirements of an adult woman was for her to be humble and have respect for her husband, elderly people, and every member of the community.
- All the children whose parents were absent had to be offered food.
- Initiation school included lessons on sex and how to maximize sexual pleasure.
- Lessons on motherhood were given.
- Initiates learned about marriage and religious ritual.

The Chisungu initiation rites, marking the transition of the initiate from childhood to adulthood and educating her on the marital, religious, and social roles of women were a central part of Bemba culture which is further discussed below.

5.3 THE CULTURAL SETTING OF THE BEMBA PEOPLE

The Bemba people are a dominant tribe in the northern part of Zambia. According to the 2011 census, Zambia comprises seventy-three ethnic groups of which the Bemba tribe is the largest. The Bemba speaking people are found in Northern Luapula and Muchinga provinces.[14] In addition, Bemba is spoken by the entire population of the Copperbelt and the central provinces of Zambia.[15] There is little specialisation in the Bemba economy. The making of pottery is the only craft exclusively for women.[16] This implies that gender hierarchy does not feature much in matters of economy in traditional Bemba society.

The social, political, and religious conditions of the Bemba have changed considerably since the 19th century. Early written information about the Bemba people comes from missionaries and western anthropologists such as Audrey Richards.[17] However, if used to interpret the social and religious systems of the Bemba people this material needs to be carefully scrutinized. The social and religious life of the Bemba were organised slightly different from how early missionaries and anthropologists describe it.

King Chitimukulu during a ukusefya pa Ngwena ceremony

There is a significant religious dimension to all community activities in traditional Bemba society. Marriage is seen as a spiritual as well as a social institution. When a marriage ceremony is preceded by Chisungu initiation, the couple is given a small pot, used for ceremonial cleansing after sexual intercourse. This indicates that sexual relations in marriage have a spiritual and ritual significance.Sex in marriage is governed by taboos. Sex is, for example, forbidden during menstruation and during socially significant events such as death and burial. While menstruating or pregnant the wife is not allowed to do certain duties such as cooking. This taboo is linked to purity concerns, and, in addition, it provides a woman with opportunities to take some rest in times of stress or sickness.

Adultery and polygamy are strongly discouraged. The death of a woman during childbirth is believed to result from adultery committed by one of the marriage partners. Once the guilty person has been identified by divination, compensation has to be offered to the innocent partner. In pre-colonial Bemba society, a husband would be executed for causing his pregnant wife's death.[18] Polygamous marriage arrangements were only allowed where levirate marriage was deemed necessary. Levirate marriage involved ritual sex with, and inheritance of, the surviving spouse by a member of the dead partner's family. This custom has proved dangerous in the context of HIV and AIDS.[19]

In Bemba society, succession follows the matrilineal line. The position of a woman in the clan structure is, therefore, much more favourable than that of a man. The birth of a girl is considered to be a blessing and a sign of approval of the marriage by the ancestors. In pre-colonial days, women acted as guardians of the shrines (babenye).[20] Some women also held positions as chiefs, showing that women could access leadership ranks in Bemba society.

It is evident from written information that Christianity and western anthropologists have contributed to misconceptions concerning the Bemba culture. The Bemba worldview and values are expressed in symbols which have never been fully described or explored.

Furthermore, Christians have remained unaware of the ritual significance of Bemba marital relationships.

Garvey points out that in their eagerness to define similarities between the Bemba God (Lesa) and the Judeo-Christian understanding of God, the missionaries have overlooked the traditional feminine features of Lesa.[21] He argues that by their attempt to adopt some aspects of the Bemba perception of God, the missionaries made it more difficult for Bemba women to master the essence of the Christian God. Some missionaries write that Bemba people used the word Lesa in both curses and praises. Similarly, anthropologists such as Richards and La Fontaine mention that vulgar language is used in the Chisungu initiation ceremony.[22] However, this is a misconception arising from a lack of understanding of the Bemba system of honour and praises. Praises among the Bemba people have a meaning that goes beyond the actual words used.

Writing about Bemba culture, Richards states that "the father is the head of an extended family whether he lives in his wife's village, in his mother's brother's family, or has managed to start a small community of his own."[23] Contrary to Richards' Eurocentric interpretation, the wife was the head of the family in traditional Bemba society.[24] The first wife of the king in Bemba society has powers equal to those of the king. It is also worthwhile noting that women who are tutors during initiation rites have more powers and command higher respect than men.

Richards alludes to the Bemba queen's position when she writes that Bemba women acted as chiefs or village 'headmen' and that women in positions of power wielded political authority but were regarded as chiefs with feminine attributes such as gentleness and hospitality.[25]

What goes almost unnoticed in her analysis is that in Bemba society any good leader including the king is expected to exhibit such feminine attributes.[26] Richards states that women were also in charge of ancestral shrines, except during political functions and that the senior wives of chiefs (*mukolo*)[27] were highly honoured.[28]

It is evident that while there are some elements of patriarchy in Bemba culture, Christianity and western influences have largely contributed to the elimination of those elements that were life-giving to women. This process of elimination has not only occurred in the actual lived experience of Bemba people but also in the subsequent representation and documenting of their cultural lives. Mercy Oduyoye points out that,

> It is still debatable whether or not the influence of Christianity has been beneficial to the socio-cultural transformation of Africa – and I am most concerned with its effects on women. It seems that sexist elements of western culture have simply fuelled the cultural sexism of traditional African society. Christian anthropology has consistently contributed to this. African men, at home with androcentrism and patriarchal order of biblical cultures, have felt their views confirmed by Christianity.[29]

Given that in a traditional Bemba cultural setting every community function has a religious and social significance, the form and practice of the Chisungu initiation rites confirm the religious and social leadership roles of women.

5.4 FORM AND PRACTICE

Chisungu initiation rites take place in two stages. The first stage is performed when a girl reaches puberty immediately after her first menstruation. In modern times this ritual lasts two to four days. The girl receives instruction on relevant issues such as cleanliness during menstruation and how to dress up. The second ritual follows prior to her marriage when she is instructed on matters pertaining to womanhood, marriage, sexuality, and her social and religious roles.[30] The ceremony can be organised for one or more initiates.

The Chisungu initiation ceremony precedes the marriage initiation ceremony. In pre-colonial times it would last between three and six months. Currently, it is performed in two to seven days. The length of the initiation depends on the family's interest in the tradition, the available resources, and on other demands on the initiate's time such as school attendance. The lessons and the format of the ceremony follow that of an indigenous marriage ceremony but in a shortened form.[31] The teachings provided to the initiates during Chisungu initiation at puberty and in the marriage initiation ceremony follow the same patterns.

Plans for the Chisungu ceremony are initiated by the parents of the initiate. They provide for the cost of the ceremony, assisted by relatives of the bridegroom-to-be.[32] The parents invite the initiation tutors (*bana chimbusa*) to arrange the ceremony and conduct the teaching. The tutors are women who are well schooled in Bemba culture and marriage customs. They have political power and are treated with great respect in the community.[33] The senior tutor is assisted by a deputy (*nakalamba*). Together they ensure that the ceremony is well organised.

5.4.1 Pre-colonial form and practice

In pre-colonial times, Chisungu initiation rites were conducted when girls had their first menstruation (*ichisungu chakubalilapo*).[34] The rites continued at the time of their second menstruation (*ukubwekesha ichisungu*). Rituals were also performed when a woman menstruated for the first time after giving birth (*ukubalwila/ukutamwina*). The first woman to see the menstrual blood of a girl became her first initiation tutor and was called *nakalamba*.

The parents of a girl who had begun menstruating prepared available food and informed the initiation tutors. The women in the community would take the girl into the bush, covering her and ululating. In the bush, the initiate sat under an *umubwilili* or *mufungo* tree, called female trees because of their significance in women's fertility rituals. The initiate would face the east. The first tutor of initiation cut small pieces of the bark of the tree so that they fell on the initiate. Thereafter, the initiate turned to face west while the tutor of initiation continued cutting bark. Finally, the tutor collected any pieces that had jumped upwards (*ubuseneme*) and pounded them to a powder which she took with the initiate to a camp fire.

Near the camp fire the women present would line up next to a small shelter made of leaves and small branches (*ichinsakwa*). The first initiation tutor and the initiate had to jump half naked over the shelter (*bafwelefye umumbatata*). The tutor jumped first, followed by the initiate, and if the initiate was known in the community as a stubborn person, the other women would whip her. This ritual indicated that the initiate had crossed over from childhood to adulthood.

The initiate had to enter the shelter that she had jumped over and was covered with leaves. The women dug small holes around the shelter in which they buried different types of seeds. This symbolized that, as a good woman, the initiate was expected to do farm work to produce food. The women set traps (*inyono*) at the entrance to the shelter. They then did beat on drums while dancing and unearthing the buried seeds:

Tulepala cibale tulepala	We are digging Chibale
Tulepala ubwekanga chibale	We are digging like Guinea Fowl
Tulepala chibale tulepala	We are digging Chibale
Tulepala ubwekanga chibale	We are digging like Guinea Fowl

While singing they removed the traps and the tutor would lead the initiate out of the shelter. If the initiate was known for stubbornness the tutor would pinch her thighs. Such mockery was a way of letting the initiate know that adult life would present her with many challenges that she had to endure, sometimes without any help. Tutor and initiate now roasted or fried the pounded bark, using two sticks, one from the *mupundu* and the other from the *mufungo* tree. The *mufungo* and *mupundu* trees are fruit bearing and, therefore, symbols of fertility. Next, the powder was mixed with castor oil and applied to the entire body of the initiate, thus removing the potential dangers posed by her menstrual blood. Menstrual blood was believed to be dangerous because it contains life. The initiate was now led through the bush and different herbs and medicines, important in female health care, were pointed out to her. The ritual continued with the tutors hanging white beads on the branch of a short *mufungo* tree. The initiate has to retrieve the beads by climbing the tree backwards, then turn around and collect the beads using her mouth while the women were singing.

Fulwe tanina,
Leelo nanina kumukolobondo.
Fulwe tanina,
Leelo nanina kumukolobondo.

> The tortoise does not climb trees
> Today it has climbed the mukolobondo tree
> The tortoise does not climb trees
> Today it has climbed the mukolobondo tree

This part of the ceremony was aimed at teaching the initiate to be strong during sexual intercourse and when faced with other hurdles in life. The initiate was now inspected, her menstrual blood was looked at, and the labia were checked to see if she had stretched them. Thereafter, she was covered and all returned to the village while singing:

Mwinjebela bantu bandi	Don't tell people
Nachisungu aibe mpwa	The initiate has stolen eggplants
Mwinjebela bantu bandi	Don't tell people
Nachisungu aibe mpwa	The initiate has stolen eggplants

Alternatively they would sing:

Mwana nakula nabobola akabomboo!	The child has reached puberty!
Tulye mbuto shabanyina,	Let us eat her mother's seeds,
Tulye mbuto shabanyina,	Let us eat her mother's seeds,
Tulye mbuto shabanyina.	Let us eat her mother's seeds.

At the initiate's house they stood, singing, ululating, and waving branches of trees. The tutor approached the door carrying the basket of medicine on her head while the women sang:

Mayo ntuule ntundu	Mother remove the load from my head,
Fili muntundu fyalema	The load is too heavy.
Mayo ntuule ntundu	Mother remove the load from my head,
Fili muntundu fyalema	The load is too heavy.

At that moment the mother of the initiate would come outside, give the tutor white beads, and remove the basket from her head. Thereafter, the women entered the house backwards while singing:

Twingile shani ee	How shall we enter?
Twingile musense nga bakolwe	Let us enter like monkeys
Twingile shani ee	How shall we enter
Twingile musense nga bakolwe	Let us enter like monkeys

In the house, they knelt down in two lines touching each other. The initiate stood on their hands and the women sang:

Umwana wamfumu uyo	There comes the daughter of the king
Pakatanta ncenjele	On the bridge
Mulemusenda bwino	Carry her well
Pakatanta ncenjele	On the bridge

The text implies that she had to look carefully after her virginity – as carefully as one crosses a bridge. At this moment the initiate touched the pillar in the room, and she would start swinging and swaying to and fro. The women sang:

Tumutemyetemye	Let us swing her
Mwansa-kabinga umulwani wauma	The devil the enemy
Tumutemyetemye	Let us swing her
Mwansa-kabinga umulwani wauma	The devil the enemy

This, too, was a symbolic lesson teaching the initiate to endure hardship in life. A paternal aunt would now put a present on a stool and the initiate would sit on top of it. Food was distributed and after the meal the tutor soaked the medicine – the powdered bark - in a container. The initiate had to wash her hands and face in this medicine every morning for a week.

During that week she remained inside. She had to sit leaning against the wall so that no one could pass her from behind. Other taboos that she had to observe included the following: she was not allowed to eat with people, to cook, make a fire, touch children or beat them lest the menstrual blood contaminated the children and make them suffer chronic coughing (*ichifuba cha mankowesha*). Lessons continued in the evening when the initiate was taught about sex and how to prevent having sex before marriage (delaying the sex debut). It was emphasized that premarital sex would cause her to suffer from chronic slimming illness, (*ubulwele bwakondoloka*) and that, besides, losing her virginity or falling pregnant before marriage would cause shame to her family and herself.

After one week, early in the morning, the initiate would be taken to the stream to bathe and to use the medicine of which afterwards the rest was by the tutor poured into the stream. The initiate continued bathing until sunset while other women were warming themselves by the fire. The bathing symbolically removed the dangerous aspects of menstruation. It represented purification and it freed the initiate from bad luck and negative omens. After sunset the tutor helped the initiate to leave the water. Her legs and hands were bound with grass and she was covered with a reed mat. Two or four women carried her on their heads back to her mother's house. All the way they kept pouring water on her while singing:

Muchingileni mayo ee muchingileni	Cover her cover her
Naine nyina alinchingile.	I was also covered by her mother
Muchileni mayo ee muchingileni	Cover her cover her
Naine nyina alichingile	I was also covered by her mother

The song reminded her that, whatever was done to her, happened in good faith and that everyone on reaching puberty had to go through the same ceremony. At the initiate's home, her paternal aunt handed presents to the tutors after which the initiate was untied. All entered the house and cooked stiff pap (*ubwali*) which was eaten by the initiate and the first initiation tutor together. On the final day of the initiation, late in the afternoon, the women gathered once more at the initiate's house for the presenting of gifts (*ukushikula*). They ate and they continued singing and dancing. The initiate and the first tutor applied castor oil and sat down on the reed mat in the middle of the gathering. Women gave presents to the initiate delivering short speeches. Some praised her for her good behaviour and told her to keep it up while others might rebuke her for bad manners, advising her to change. Some women gave her seeds and other items that would help her to be a good agriculturist. So came the initiation rites for the first menstruation to an end. The ceremonies continued at the time of the second menstruation. When the second menstruation began the initiate informed the first tutor. They would go into the bush and repeat the ritual meant to remove the dangerous aspects of the menstrual blood. Thereafter, the mother brewed beer. When the beer was ready, women gathered at the initiate's house to celebrate and to continue teaching the initiate through dancing, songs, and proverbs. The grandmother or the first tutor would interpret the meaning of the songs and the proverbs for the initiate. She also learned different types of dances.

If she was already engaged, the Chisungu rites would involve the groom. After the second menstruation the initiate was referred to as *Nachisungu* (the nubile bride) and the groom became *Lumbwe* (the groom of the nubile bride). On the last day of the ceremony, following the second menstruation the groom was invited by the tutors (*banachimbusa*) into the initiate's house.[35]

There were variations to this component of the rites. If the initiate was not engaged, this part of the rites was performed during the marriage initiation ceremony. In any case, the groom had to perform this ritual before the wedding ceremony.

He carried a bundle of firewood, salt, and meat and was accompanied by his sister or any other female relative. The bundle of firewood was untied while some elderly women danced in honour of the relative who accompanied him. Thereafter, the groom left the house. The *nakalamba* (an assistant tutor) now handed two undressed chickens to the *nachimbusa* (senior tutor) and the bride. They plucked their chickens to prepare them for cooking. The groom was invited to come back with his relatives, and he would perform a ritual called *ukulasa imbusa*, shooting the sacred marriage emblem or *mushintililo*.

The emblem, made with a mixture of clay and charcoal, and attached to the wall of the initiate's house, was shot by the groom with a bow and arrow provided by his relatives. Underneath the marriage emblem the bride was seated. If his shot was successful it meant that he would be a worthy husband. If he failed to hit the emblem, he was mocked by the tutors for being a useless husband before they allowed him to make another attempt. After succeeding, the groom would shoot at other emblems or jump over them.[36] The rituals now came to an end. If the initiate was engaged there would still be a food-giving ceremony (*amatebeto*) and the women would sing:

Sekeseke twakupandila	We have plied
Niwe mwiine ukayonene	It is now up to you
Sekeseke twakupandila	We have plied
Niwe mwiine ukayonene	It is now up to you

'We have plied' implies 'we have left you a virgin' and it is up to you to observe the lessons and preserve your virginity. If you go wrong, don't blame anyone.

5.4.2 Colonial and post-colonial rituals

Already in colonial times the initiation ceremony had been shortened to two months, but the rites continue to consist of a sequence of events. First, the initiation tutors isolate the initiate in the initiation house and lessons are given using song and dance as teaching media. On the second day, she is taken into the bush where she has to sit under the *mufungo* or the *mubwilili* tree, and from sunrise to sunset dancing and singing women continue her education.[37] The following few days marriage or sacred emblems (*imbusa*) are designed as well as 'things to be handed down'.[38] Different marriage emblems are drawn on the walls of the initiation house. The presentation and explanation of the emblems take place in the night of the last day of the initiation.

The sacred emblems are of various types, but all are considered to be secret in the sense that they have either a secret name or a secret meaning according to Bemba traditions. At the end of the training the initiate is presented to the community. She displays the dancing skills she has acquired during her seclusion and she receives presents.[39]

The role of the initiation tutors is to teach the initiate on the essential roles of women as providers of life. The tuition formally introduces the initiate to adult life. Some lessons focus on good behaviour towards parents, neighbours, and elderly people. Other teachings discuss negative role models that should not be emulated. The lessons are conveyed using songs, dancing, and marriage emblems. The young women are also taught about the mysteries surrounding menstrual blood that has to be handled very cautiously to protect women from infertility and witchcraft. The initiate learns to determine when menstruation is over and sexual relations can be resumed. A menstruating woman is not expected to cook or put salt on food.

Another theme of initiation tuition is to avoid premarital and extramarital sex. It is believed that premarital sex can cause a 'slimming' sickness called *ichifuba cantanda bwanga*.[40] The symptoms are similar to those of AIDS.[41] In marriage, women have to be faithful to their husbands. It is clear that much of the initiation teaching is related to marriage and sex, although sex education is certainly not the only purpose of the rites. The initiate is also taught not to sleep with men especially those older than her.[42] This could provide a useful resource in teachings on HIV prevention, for example, by abstinence and delaying the sex debut.

Part of initiation instruction is concerned with how to satisfy a man. Women are taught to feel free to initiate sex in marriage. This is quite clear from initiation songs and from the initiation solo dance. In this respect, Richards refers to "the dilemma of a matrilineal society in which men are dominant but the line goes through the women".[43] The initiate is also familiarised with the taboos governing sex. She is advised to refuse sex when she is menstruating and when she or her child is sick.[44] Fiedler rightly argues that cultural values encouraging women to exercise their power over sexual affairs need to be upheld.[45]

In the context of domestic violence and HIV and AIDS a woman can refuse to have sex with her husband if he is not prepared to use a condom. Discussing when and how to have sex should be a normal thing between husband and wife.

African women theologians have largely condemned women's strong focus on satisfying their husbands. According to them, women are turned into sex objects by their husbands which makes them more vulnerable to abuse.[46] Fiedler, however, states that men during their initiation rites are also taught to satisfy their wives in sex.[47] She adds that the dancing and the swerving of the waist during sexual intercourse satisfy both husband and wife. Similarly, Schmid describes sex as a gift from God that must be enjoyed as long as it is within a committed relationship.[48]

The initiate is taught about the functioning of body parts during sex so that she is prepared, for example, for the changing size of the man's penis when he is ready for sex. It is important that, in the context of domestic violence and HIV and AIDS, the silence about sex is broken. As Schmid points out, talking about sex and anything related to it should not be taboo.[49]

In Chisungu initiation, the initiate is inspected to see if she has stretched the labia. Pulling of the labia is encouraged so that the husband can play with them and to tighten the vagina which, along with dry sex, is thought to add pleasure to the sexual experience.[50] Fiedler sees the pulling of the labia as contributing to the stability of marriage.[51] However, Phiri points out that the stretched labia increase the vulnerability of women to HIV due to tearing of the vaginal surface during intercourse.[52]

There exist songs and emblems that teach women not to ask their husbands for sex. There also are songs and emblems that teach women not to condemn their husbands for immorality. These are, however, contradicted by other songs and emblems that empower women to rebuke their husbands for immorality and to exercise control over their sex life as will be shown in the following chapters.[53] Initiation also includes lessons on the importance of hygiene.

Celebrating the attainment of sexual and social maturity, Chisungu initiation reflects tribal attitudes to sex, marriage, and fertility. Phiri describes initiation rites as important because they give identity to women.[54] At the same time they are instructed on matters related to sex and marriage. She, however, points out that false teachings concerning the taboos related to menstruation and submission of wives to husbands should be discouraged. Fiedler adds that positive elements in African culture which empower women should be upheld while those that make women vulnerable should be discarded.[55]

5.5 CONCLUSION

Chapter five discusses the purpose of the Chisungu initiation rites and explains their form and practice against the background of Bemba culture. The initiation takes place at puberty when the girl experiences her first and second menstruation.[56] The rites mark the transition of the initiate from childhood to adulthood, educating her on matters of sex and on the social and religious leadership roles of a Bemba woman. A comparison of the rites in past and present reveals continuities and discontinuities in their structure and content.

Initiation lessons emphasize personal hygiene, especially during menstruation; taking care of the family; maximising satisfaction during sexual intercourse; social and religious roles of a woman; sticking to one sexual partner and avoiding premarital and extramarital sexual affairs. If these lessons are taught today in a way relevant to contemporary society, Chisungu initiation rites might create an opportunity for increasing women's empowerment in Zambia. The rites are presently reinvented and modified to address social issues such as poverty and HIV and AIDS. In view of attempts to reclaim Chisungu initiation rites as a response to the problems that affect women today, chapter seven will be concerned with the gendered values of the rites.

CHAPTER SIX

FUNCTION, FORM, AND PRACTICES OF BEMBA MARRIAGE RITES

6.1 INTRODUCTION

Marriage is sacred in Africa and beyond, because it solidifies relationships that enrich communities and nations by bringing forth new life and new hope. African cultures celebrate the coming of the rains, the first harvest, and the birth of a child.
—AHS Society

Marriage is a central institution in Africa that is seen as an enhancement and enrichment of the entire community. Marriage promotes sharing, tolerance, consideration, empathy, selflessness, and other virtues. It is believed that the absence of marriage symbolizes the death of a community and a people. Communities that don't recognize marriage become decadent and self-destructive and experience a range of social, economic, and health problems. Marriage initiation rites are rites of passage marking the transition from unmarried to married life. As La Fontaine notes, such rites consist of symbolic actions and have a social meaning.[1] Initiation rites are a demonstration of positions of power and social relations in a society.

6.2 PURPOSE

A man marries a woman for four reasons: for her property, for her rank, for her beauty, and for her character. So, marry the one who is best in character and prosper.

—Islamic Hadith

Ubukulu bwa Nkoko masako (The respect of a chicken lies in its feathers)

—Bemba proverb

In Bemba culture, marriage initiation rites are a continuation of Chisungu initiation rites and serve the same purposes.[2] First, marriage initiation rites celebrate the transition from unmarried to married life (*ukumucindila*). Second, marriage initiation rites provide the initiate with education (*ukufunda*) relevant to his/her marital and social roles.[3] The ritual is a communal event and bonds two people, enshrining obligations and values. These lessons are again conveyed through sacred emblems (*imbusa*) and songs.

The third purpose of marriage initiation rites is to mark the change of status and give a new identity to the initiate[4] which confirms that he/she is now in the possession of knowledge concerning marital behaviour and social etiquettes. The rites include sex education and lessons on what may be expected from a married person. The initiate is brought into the company of initiated men and women and assumes a position in the hierarchy of people who are familiar with the community's culture.

The fourth aim of marriage initiation is to offer prayers for fecundity. Parents and the entire community offer prayers for the well-being and fecundity of initiates. Marriage initiation rites also declare the union of two families, and sometimes of the two communities or tribes from where bride and groom hail. Marriage, historically, has been used in political unions between nations and between different ethnic groups to secure peace, trade, and development. The central place of marriage in African communities is one thing that unites the cultures of the continent south of the Sahara.

Marriage also provides the milieu in which human beings can enjoy sex and produce children. Having sex in the bush or unmarried persons having sex is considered an offence to the ancestors. The bearing of children guarantees the continuity of the family lineage. An additional purpose of marriage rites is to entertain (*ukusefya*) and to display social status. Dancing and drinking beer are part of the rites. Finally, marriage rites empower the groom and the bride, and the ceremony ends with the couple receiving gifts.

6.3 FORM AND PRACTICE

6.3.1 FORM AND PRACTICE IN PRE-COLONIAL TIMES
In pre-colonial Bemba society, marriage began when a man became engaged to a young girl usually below the age of puberty (*ukukobekela*).[5] Marriage was considered as a union of a man and woman for life. Divorce was accepted only in exceptional cases which included lack of respect for relatives of the spouse and barrenness. Marriage signified the coming together of the families of the bride and groom. Marriage initiation rites were performed after Chisungu initiation. When the elders noticed that the bride had reached puberty and experienced her first menstruation (*ichisungu chakubalilapo*), she was stopped from staying at the groom's house to prevent pre-marital sex. Withdrawing the girl was also a way of informing the groom that the girl had reached

puberty.

In a matrilineal society, wedding ceremonies were held at the bride's village while in patrilineal societies, they took place in the groom's village. There were instances where two wedding ceremonies were held, one in each village. There were a few differences between the marriage of a commoner (*umuntu yaweyawe*) and a member of the royal family (*uwakubufumu*). It was desirable to marry someone belonging to a good family. A good family was industrious, hospitable, and without a record of witchcraft. The engagement price was a man's way of showing he was serious. It was common practice among the Bemba people to betroth girls at an early age and sometimes even unborn children were betrothed. However, the issue of early marriage did not arise due to the social and economic situation at the time. In today's society, marrying before one is eighteen years of age is not acceptable.

6.3.1. 1 Engagement

The engagement, celebrated with ritual, was the first step in the marriage process. Marriage was initiated by a man's family. When the family judged that it was time for the man to become engaged he would visit another village hoping to find a bride. The village elders would ask him what he was looking for. In the late afternoon, they would invite young ladies one by one and the man would indicate a girl he liked. This girl would be asked back in the evening when the man proposed love. He then returned to his village. Now the family would appoint an intermediary (*shibukombe* or *nabukombe*). Alternately, parents could choose a girl for their son to marry, sometimes without consulting her. Some parents might consult the man if he was old enough to marry. The arrangements for the engagement were made by the parents. If the family accepted his choice, an intermediary represented the family in finalizing the arrangements.[6] The intermediary was chosen from among respected men or women in the community who were familiar with Bemba traditions (*ifimbusa*). When all was set for the engagement, the parents would reserve money[7] for the betrothal (*insalamo/ubusonge*) and say the following words:

> *Wecuma chandi uli buulungu taupita apali akafundo. Nga chakuti nachiyana ukuti umwana wandi engile ilya nganda,bayekupokelela amaboko yabili. Nga taciligile umo imipashi yesu yishibile uyebwela* / My wealth you are like beads that cannot go through a knot. If it is fine to marry from that family, let them accept you. But if it's not according to our ancestors, let them reject you.

The next step was to send the intermediary to the girl's family to negotiate on behalf of the groom. An engagement present was put in a basket made of reeds (*icipe*), and the intermediary would visit the girl's parents at dusk. He was welcomed with the words: *Mwaisen mukwai, ukulichi uko mwafuba?* (Welcome, how are you?) The intermediary put the basket on the ground and unfolded the news: *Mukwai ndefwaya ukukakila* (I have come to engage your daughter.) As he represented the groom, the intermediary spoke as if he was the one marrying. The father of the girl or his representative would accept the basket and ask the intermediary to come for the answer at a later date after which the family of the girl would sit down to decide whether to accept or refuse the proposal. If the answer was 'yes,' other steps in the marriage process followed.

The next step involved the groom building a house in the bride's village. The groom and the bride now could meet at the house of the bride's grandmother. The groom could only eat or bathe at his parents-in-law's place after a food offering ceremony (*ichilanga mulilo* or *amatebeto*) had taken place. His food would be prepared by the girl's grandmother or sister. After a week the groom sent the intermediary with a small present to his future in-laws to ask them for work to do (*ukwipusha imilimo*). The bride's family made food for the groom as long as he was working in their fields. But the groom was not allowed to eat the first food which was stiff pap with chicken (*ubwali bwa nkoko*) made by his mother-in-law. Instead, the groom would ask his elderly female relatives to come and collect the food and present it to another family to eat. Thereafter, the food for the groom would be prepared by the bride's grandmother or elder sisters. The groom was free to ask the source of the food every time it was brought to him.

When the groom started working (*ukulomba imilimo*) for his in-laws, he was joined by the intermediary and some male relatives. They never knocked off without being given a small gift by the bride's parents. On subsequent days the groom worked on his own, stopping when he wanted to and without getting presents. He was given any work that the in-laws wanted to be done from cultivating a field to building a house. In that way, the in-laws tested the groom in various ways to make sure of his capabilities. Every action undertaken by the in-laws had a purpose. If, for example, they put too much salt in his food, they were making sure that he wasn't impotent.

With the engagement, courtship began (*ukwishisha*). The bride started behaving like a wife and would perform family duties when she visited the groom. These included washing, sweeping, cooking, and drawing water. She was not allowed to talk to the groom, cook, or enter his house the first time she came to his place until he had given her a small present (*ukushikula*). She would normally be escorted by a little girl to avoid suspicions of having committed fornication especially after she had reached puberty. The groom, similarly, began to behave like a husband by taking good care of her in addition to doing work at his in-law's place.

The period of courtship served to make sure the choice of bride or groom was the right one. If the family decided against the selected partner, the engagement could be broken off, hence, the Bemba proverb, *Nkobekelwa te chupo* (engagement is not formal marriage). Breaking an engagement when an impediment to marriage had been identified was acceptable. This does not mean that in traditional Bemba society a man could break an engagement at will. R. M. Kambole notes that the notion of an engagement as not necessarily binding implied that an engaged couple had to respect those who were not engaged as it is God only who determines one's destiny.[8] The groom and the bride were monitored to make sure they strictly followed social norms. Breaking off an engagement brought shame on the family of the bride or groom, depending on who initiated the break-up. Parents of the bride would usually return the engagement present (*insalamu*) to the groom's family, indicating that their daughter was free again and could get married to any other man coming her way.

6.3.1. 2 Food-giving ceremony

The food ceremony (*amatebeto/icilanga mulilo*) followed.[9] From the first day of the engagement until Chisungu initiation rites the groom had been observing food taboos. But now the intermediary offered the bride's family a present with the request that the groom be allowed to eat food prepared by his mother-in-law: *mukwai umwana wabene alaonda ku nsala,* meaning "the child of our beloved is wasting with hunger." In pre-colonial times the food-giving ceremony took place six months after the the engagement date or three months after the initiation ceremony. The groom was now thought to have proven that he did work hard, was well-behaved, and is able to look after the extended family. The different foods prepared during the ceremony included fish (*isabi*), local polony (*chikanda*), okra (*umulembwe*), pumpkin seeds (*impupu*), caterpillar (*ifishimu*), beans (*chilemba*), groundnuts (*imbalala*), and beer (*katubi*). The bride's family offered the groom with his food a present and a bowl of water as a symbolic invitation to eat and bath at their place.

The intermediary, surrounded by the food, welcomed the arrival of relatives of the groom. Elderly members of the bride's family, her initiation tutors (*banachimbusa*), and some close friends of the groom would also attend the ceremony. An elderly woman related to the bride or an initiation tutor would, under much joking, explain the significance of each food in Bemba culture. If there was any food that the groom did not eat he would point it out to inform his in-laws.[10] Without failure, the meal included a whole chicken with its gizzard next to it on a plate, symbolizing the welcome extended by the bride's family in a spirit of humility. Game meat on the menu could be duiker (*impombo*) or eland. Wild pig (*kapoli*) was never offered. The ceremony was enlivened with humorous remarks, singing, dancing, and ululation.

After the importance of each food had been explained the women left the house. The intermediary took his present and eating started. The plates and containers with food and beer were later returned to the bride's family with double the amount of presents. After this ceremony, the groom would no more inquire after the source of food that he got from the bride's family and he was free to eat anything cooked by them. The food-giving ceremony was followed by the wedding ceremony. In some families, the food-giving ceremony was held before the Chisungu rites so that the groom was able to eat freely while working for his in-laws.

6.3.1. 3 Request for the wedding

After the food offering ceremony, the groom's family sent the intermediary to the bride's parents with a present (*icilomba*) indicating that the groom was now ready to marry. This was the second present after the engagement price (*insalamo*). If the bride's parents agreed, the groom's parents would send the intermediary once more to the bride's house (again with a present or *icipuula*) informing them that they wished for a full wedding (*ubwinga*) and not a kind of shortened ceremony (*ichombela nganda*). When everyone was in agreement the bride's family decided on the price (*ubwimashi*) to be paid by the groom. The price was symbolically referred to as virginity money. The amount was shared equally between the bride's father and mother. After the groom had paid virginity money he sent the intermediary to the bride's parents to ask for the bride price (*impango*). The bride price was a composite sum consisting of *icipapa nabwinga* (the value of the girl having been raised by the mother) and expenses made for clothing, feeding, beds and mats, and teaching (*inyemba, ifukafuka, impasa, inkula*). Today, the bride price would also include the cost of her education. The sum would be refundable if the woman did not conceive in marriage.

The bride's family usually gathered to decide the bride-price or lobola (*impango*). This was the main payment associated with marriage in Bemba culture. The bride-price included two to three large cloths (*ifilundu*) and a few other items mentioned above. No animals were part of the bride price among the Bemba people. After the groom had paid part of the bride-price, the intermediary asked on his behalf for the wedding date to be set: *mukwai bankake amaboko, bansheko amolu*

("Kindly tie me by hands; leave the legs so I can move around and look for the remaining amount"). In many cases, more than half of the bride-price was paid before the wedding and the rest afterwards.

6.3.1. 4 Wedding ceremony

The wedding ceremony involved the performance of a number of rituals. There were three ways of getting married in pre-colonial Bemba society.

- Marriage without a wedding (*ukutolanafye*). This type of marriage was usually chosen by elderly people who had been married before, for example a widow and widower who decided to tie the knot. In such a case, there was not much festivity. This way of getting married was also followed in the case of elopements (*ukufyusha*).
- A short marriage ceremony (*ichombela nganda*). A short ceremony was preferred by a people who wished to be formally married but who were too busy or lacked the resources to have a full ceremony. This shortened form of a wedding could in modern-day terms be referred to as a white wedding without a reception. No beer was prepared. There would be some food, and the couple received a few lessons and blessings.
- A full wedding ceremony (*ubwinga bwakapundu*) with a reception, many festivities, and beer and food for the entire community.

In pre-colonial Bemba society, a wedding could take place only between a woman who was a virgin and a man. As far as the man is concerned, it did not matter, even if he had been married before. In the case of a woman who had lost her virginity, the first form of marriage (*ukutolana*) would be appropriate. If the girl had become engaged before reaching puberty, the wedding ceremony would take place a year after the engagement or three to nine months after Chisungu initiation.

Prior to the wedding both families prepared different foods and beer (*katata na katubi*). The beer had to be strong and well fermented (*tabufwile bwaba umubanga*). If the groom's family lived far from the bride's home, they would come and camp in the bride's village to facilitate the preparations. Beer was ritually significant. Without beer there could be no wedding. To start off the preparations the father of the bride blessed the millet and handed it to his sister (the bride's paternal aunt). The following day women started winnowing and pounding millet and sorghum to make the brew. They would sing:

Makubi mwee!	Vulture!
Eee!	Yes!
Mutalile?	Have you eaten?
Awee.	No.
Mupe cani?	Should I give you grass?
Awee.	No.
Mupe mbalala?	Should I give you groundnuts?
Awe.	No.
Mupe mpapa?	Should I give you the sack for the baby?
Eyaa, eyaa!	Yes, yes!
Tulimakoshi sompa.	We have long necks
Tulimakoshi sompa.	We have long necks

The women would pinch the mother and the paternal aunt of the bride. This was to remind the bride that men are difficult. If you want harmony at home, do what your husband tells you. Sometimes it is good to put the interests of others before one's own. When the millet had been pounded the mother and the bride's paternal aunt had to crawl into the house while the initiation tutors of the bride were whipping them. Women would sing:

Namwali...	Namwali.....
Yulili ngombe shingile.	Open so that cows can enter
Namwali....	Namwali.......
Shalya malembo shapita.	The cows have passed

The song conveys that sometimes a husband may leave his wife for another woman. But, if he decides to come back, kindly welcome him. He is a human being and therefore prone to making mistakes. However, he is your husband – your love. In the evening, the groom was given a pot or a calabash of beer, told to go to his parents' house and come back only after some days. The idea was to make bride and groom miss each other so that they would be doubly happy to see each other again on their wedding day. The bride, in the meantime, went to her grandmother. She had to stop bathing until the wedding day so that on the big day she would feel and look like new.

Women usually spent a day or two preparing marriage emblems. The tutors and the bride's mother collected medicine, white soil (*impemba*), red soil, and soil of other colours in the bush which were applied to sacred marriage emblems (*imbusa*). They made clay figurines and drew emblems on the walls of the house where the marriage initiation took place. They also drew emblems on a bamboo basket (*ulupe*) and prepared a place for the bride and groom to sit during the ceremony.

On the afternoon before the wedding day young girls took the bamboo basket with the emblems, a bow and an arrow, and started singing:

Cilende	Loose woman

Kumbwe tete kubanobe kumbwe tete	See the straw from your friends
Cilende	Loose woman
Kumbwe tete kubanobe kumbwe tete	See the straw from your friends

With the bow and arrow they started prodding the girl who carried the bamboo basket singing:

Seeya ee!	Seeya
Yangayo	Celebrate
Bamulasa!	They have struck her
Pacikwembe	On the cloth

The text points to the importance of sex. The bow and arrow symbolize the husband and his penis. The bamboo basket symbolizes the wife and her vagina.

In the evening, the bride was taken from her grandmother to her mother's house. The women sang:

Tucitwale uko bacibashile,	Let us take her where she was made
Wecinkolobondo.	You good for nothing
Tuchitwale uko bacibashile,	Let us take her where she was made
Wecinkolobondo.	You good for nothing

This was the last time the bride would spend the night at her parents' place. Early in the morning, the women came to see if she was well and ready for the wedding. Sometimes overanxious brides would fall ill on their wedding day. The bride's mother offered the women a calabash of beer after which they dispersed.

During the ceremony, many songs were sung. Each contained a

meaningful lesson for the bride. Some songs were hard to interpret, and it was the responsibility of her first initiation tutor, her paternal aunt, and her grandmother to explain the texts to the bride. The bride's grandfather, uncle, or the intermediary would interpret the songs for the groom. While preparing the wedding food women would sing:

Peemba, peemba,	Wait, wait,
Panama tapashima moto panama.	Don't put out fire when cooking meat
Peemba, peemba.	Wait, wait
Panama tapashima moto panama.	Don't put out fire when cooking meat.

This implied that a woman has to present her husband, children, and visitors with good food. It would be foolish (bupuumbu) to neglect this duty.

While women picked up white ceremonial beads with their mouths, passing them on to the person next to them, right around the entire circle, they sang:

Cembe wemusha,	Eagle,
Wayipama peshiba lyakwe wayipamapo.	You have thrown yourself into the river
Cembe wemusha,	Eagle,
Wayipama peshiba lyakwe wayipamapo.	You have thrown yourself into the river

They would alternatively sing:

Ala aka kumulomo	This is from the mouth
Sotole cembe sobuulee	Eagle come and get it.
Ala aka kumulomo	This is from the mouth
Sotole cembe sobuulee	Eagle come and get it.

The eagle represented the groom and male genitalia. The calabash of beer and the river symbolized the bride and her genitalia. Throwing oneself into the river stood for having sexual intercourse. White beads symbolized the child that might result. Passing the white beads around meant that children have to be treasured. If God blesses one with a child, one should look well after it.

The bridegroom had returned to the bride's place two or three days before the wedding to join in the preparations.[11] In some pre-colonial Bemba communities, wedding celebrations were opened by the initiation tutors who would give the groom a whip to whip the bride on the back. The idea was to teach the bride that in marriage a woman may be beaten. Should wife and husband fight, they should not involve the community. Also, the wife should not deny the husband sex just because they quarreled or fought. Sex should always be a privilege (kutombanafye).

A day after his arrival, female initiation tutors would take the bride into the bush for lessons on sex and motherhood while male tutors taught the groom, also in the bush, about sex and family life. The instruction was thorough. They were also familiarized with different herbs and medicines important for concerns such as fertility and parenthood. If the groom proved stubborn, he was mocked and beaten, and tutors would make him carry a log of firewood from the bush to his in-law's house. Similarly, if the bride was stubborn, she would be ridiculed and beaten, and she would have to carry a big load of firewood to her mother's place. Well-behaved brides and grooms were not mocked. Rituals continued in the village. In the late afternoon, the bride was taken to the groom's house. The groom would light a stick (umwenge) and move it above the bride's head as a symbol of best wishes. The tutors then shaved bride and groom (ukubabeya amaso).

Female tutors shaved the armpits and genitalia of the bride while male tutors shaved the groom's armpits and private parts. Thereafter, castor oil was applied to their bodies.

The shaving of private parts (*ukubeya amaso*) is important in Bemba culture. A couple is responsible for shaving each other's private parts, and finding that the private parts of one's spouse had already been shaved was a serious offense and indicated that adultery had been committed—a possible reason for divorce. If one of the spouses had committed adultery the initiation tutors would announce: *Pano pa ng'anda napaluba amaso,* or "We have lost pubic hair at this home." Partners had to ensure that the other's private parts were clean. Widows and widowers were mocked if their spouse had died with long pubic hair.[12]

In the evening, the initiation tutors brought beer (*ubwalwa bwacifunda-bwinga*) and continued teaching groom and bride, first, separately and, thereafter, together. Female tutors taught the bride and male tutors taught the groom about female and male sexual organs and their functions. The lessons focused on how to maximize sexual pleasure and reach orgasm while avoiding hurting or injuring each other during intercourse. Tutors would tell the man: *Wilapupumina ukaicena nangu ukuchena umwanakashi,* meaning "Be patient and gentle so as not to bruise your penis or the woman's vagina." They would also say: *Ubwamba bufwile buleluma pakuti nga waposa amenshi yaleuma kumusana wakwa namayo aleumfwako nobukali* or "The penis should be strong enough so that when you ejaculate the sperm it hits the woman's vagina with force." The groom was told that during sexual intercourse he should spill some sperm on the bed by withdrawing so that the tutors could make sure that he was a real man.

The bride was taught, sometimes in the house of her paternal aunt or *nyina senge,* on the rituals of family life and on her religious and social leadership roles as a married woman. Much of the lessons were a revision of teaching offered during the initiation rites but with a stronger emphasis on sexuality and motherhood. Women received more lessons than men because of their biological set up and their social and religious responsibilities in Bemba culture. There was also instruction on how in a natural way to effect a spacing of pregnancies, in other words, family planning. At the end of the lessons the bride returned to her mother's house singing:

Akebo banjebele,	What I was told to do,
Nacita.	I have done.
Nga kuli kambi,	If there is something more I need to do,
Ba njebe.	Please tell me.

This means that the bride had been thoroughly informed. Around midnight she was stripped, and the tutors covered her in the smoke of a fragrant plant so that she would smell nice. They gave her an inhalant (*bamufutikila*) and painted her body with castor oil. From childhood onward, girls wore a girdle of amulets (*impimpi*) and beads (*ubulungu*) around their waist. It was thought that the girdle would make the waist curve in a way attractive to men. The tutors now removed the childhood beads and amulets and gave her new beads (*chisasa*) to put on. Her paternal aunt carried her naked on her back, covered with a cloth provided by the groom, to the house where the groom was waiting for her and for their first sexual meeting (consummation of the marriage).[13] The groom and the intermediary received her with presents. Her initiation tutors and some elderly women accompanied her, dancing and singing:

Nse nse	Nse nse
Tubatwalile, tubatwalile	Let us take her to them
Nse nse o	Nse nse o
Tubatwalile abene bakayonawile	Let us take her to them, so they can spoil her by themselves

The women let it be known that they have brought a virgin and what happens to her afterwards is the business of the bride and groom. At the groom's house the bride was put on a reed mat or a bed covered with a whitish cloth. The intermediary sat next to the groom and explained the proceedings. The groom gave the bride and the paternal aunt a present while the initiation tutors embarked on more lessons. The bride's paternal aunt or her grandmother handed over a sack (*ichipe*) containing items deemed necessary for married life. In the sack were red, white, and black beads, a sewing needle, castor oil (*amafuta ya mono*), a container, and so on. The wife would wear red beads if she wanted to inform her husband that she was menstruating. The black beads indicated that menstruating had finished. White beads meant that she was ovulating and it was the best time for sex. Red ants (*impashi*), mentioned in the lessons, also symbolized menstruation. The groom was told that his wife is the one who should close the door at night. The bride was instructed to always face her husband when sleeping. Both had to sleep naked and admire each other's nakedness. After the short teaching session, the paternal aunt commanded the groom to sleep with the bride: *Tata twamiletela umwana uyu mumutombe* ("We have brought the bride, deflower her."). The aunt, tutors and relatives then left.

If the groom had successfully deflowered the bride, he would toss some hot embers outside the door. The aunt and the initiation tutors burst out into ululation. The groom had proved to be strong and virile (*te *chibola*). Some brides apparently fainted at their first glimpse of a man's penis.[14] In the morning, the new wife was interrogated by the tutors as to how many times they had made love. A real man was expected to go up to four or six rounds. The whitish cloth was checked for blood stains confirming that the bride had been a virgin. The ritual was thus a test of the groom's virility and the bride's virginity. If the groom failed to perform (*nga ni chibola*), the bride would come rushing outside. That marked the end of the wedding ceremony. Similarly, if the bride was not a virgin, the groom's family would cancel the marriage and demand repayment of the bride-price unless they had known beforehand that she wasn't a virgin. If no such problems had arisen, women outside would ululate and sing:

Wakula mayo wansanga ee,	You have grown up like me,
We mwengele wandi.	My pine tree.
Wakula mayo wansanga ee,	You have grown up like me,
We mwengele wandi.	My pine tree.

They would alternatively sing:

Munjili mwana wandi	Warthog my child
Njenje munjili mwana wandi njenje	Njenje Warthog my child njenje
Wakula twalingana njenje,	You have grown up like me njenje
Wamona ifyo namona njenje,	You have seen what I have seen njenje
Njenje njenje	Njenje njenje
Njenje munjili mwana wandi njenje	Njenje Warthog my child njenje

In other words, the bride was now fully grown up. There were no more bedroom secrets for her. She had seen and experienced what her mother had seen and experienced after her wedding.

In traditional Bemba society, a bride-price was only paid for a virgin. The loss of virginity was shameful. If her wedding was cancelled, the paternal aunt would take the bride to her mother. The chickens collected for a festive meal were set free and invited guests dispersed. Such a situation brought shame on both families. However, if the groom was virile and the bride a virgin, the wedding celebrations would continue until the next day while the bride and the groom were sleeping. The neighbourhood community participated in the festivities, drinking beer, singing, ululating, and holding dance competitions throughout the night (ukubecha).

Early the following morning (kumachacha), the tutors or an elderly member of the bride's family would lead the couple to the stream to bath (ukowa). Medicines were sprinkled onto the water and by the stream carried towards the immersed couple. It was a purification ritual aimed at removing the bad luck of premarital life. The couple would find the house where they had spent the night, and the reed mat or the bed on which they had slept, freshly cleaned. The old fire had been cleared away and three old men made preparations for a new fire using fire sticks. The fire would be made between three 'pillars' (amafwesa).

This is the moment when the cooking ritual (ukuteka akalongo) was performed.[15] The couple could now start cooking food to feed themselves and their visitors. The paternal aunt arrived with the marriage pot (akalongo) and a gourd of castor oil (insupa ya mafuta ya mono). She made the new fire near the foot of the bed or mat between three little anthill-shaped pillars or supports (amafwesa) for the marriage pot filled with water. The aunt and the newly-wed couple lifted the little pot together, holding it by its edge between thumb and first finger and put it on the fire. When the water was warm, the aunt put a little in a basin and poured it over the fingers of groom and bride. The purpose was again the purification of the couple. It was believed that without this ritual the couple would die of poisoning, contamination, or consumption (*ukukowela*).

For the traditional virginity and virility meal ritual (*ubwali ne nkonko shachisungu*) the bride's paternal aunt cooked stiff pap, stirring with a cooking stick made from a branch of a female tree (*mufungo* or *mupundu*), with chicken and roasted meat for the couple's breakfast. The aunt washed their hands while singing:

Kasambe umulume wecinangwa,	Go wash your husband you worthless person,
Chibale, Chibale.	Chibale, Chibale.
Napanshi ulaala wecinangwa,	And the floor where you sleep,
Chibale, Chibale.	Chibale, Chibale.

These words emphasized that it was the bride who was responsible for cleaning the husband's private parts after sexual intercourse using her hands. She was also expected to kneel or roll down and thank him for a job well done. It was her task to keep the bedroom, the house, her husband, herself, and their close environment clean. A wife who was dirty was considered foolish. As the initiation tutors emphasized: *Ulekwata ubusaka, umwakashi uununka panyo kabili tasamba no mulumo chipuba* or "Be clean, a woman whose private parts stink and who does not clean her husband is foolish."

The bride's paternal aunt would take small lumps of food (*ulutoshi*) and feed husband and wife until the meal was over. Thereafter, she took the liver of a hen, given to the couple by the bride's family, and the gizzard of a cock, presented by the groom's family, and she touched these to the lips of bride and groom. The little marriage pot remained on the hearth until the fire went out and the aunt would remove the pot only after the couple had given her a piece of bark cloth (*ichilundu/ichitenge*). She would put another small pot in its place for the couple to use in their married life.[16]

Next, the aunt took a little stiff pap to rub it over the bodies of groom and bride after which she anointed them with castor oil (*amafuta ya mono*). The marriage pot (*akolongo kachupo*) was used whenever the couple had sex. Together they would fill the pot with water, put it on the fire, and wash their hands in warm water in a ritual of purification. It was feared that they might contaminate young people if they did not wash their hands in water from the marriage pot. An important taboo was that a person who had committed adultery should not touch the marriage pot. The pot thus fulfilled a role in preventing adultery. The wedding procedure, from the early ritual in the river to the making of new fire, symbolized the beginning of a new life blessed with fecundity.

The bride's paternal aunt kept the ashes (*imito*) of the fire and the leftover dry pieces of pap (*inkokotolo*). They were buried together with the wedding stick brushes and the pubic hair of groom and bride under a mufungo or a mupundu tree. If the bride would fail to conceive she would pour fertility medicine onto the place where these items were buried.

In the afternoon, the bridal couple, dressed beautifully, sat on a reed mat outside for the giving ceremony (*ukuluula/ukushikula*). Facing the gathered members of the community they received small gifts and last-minute advice on married life from parents, relatives, friends, and well-wishers. The father of the bride was the first to offer both a gift and some advice followed by her mother and other close relatives.

Thereafter, the groom's family offered both a gift and some advice. Next, the father of the bride presented the groom with a spear saying: *Tata namipela ili fumo, umwaume onse uukafwaya ukwngala ku mukashi wenu mukamulase nokumwipaya* ("I give you this arrow. If any man steals or seduces your wife, shoot and kill him.") Sometimes, instead of a spear, a bow and arrow were given. Gifts had meaning and were useful. There would be an axe and a hoe for agriculture, fishing nets, spears for hunting, and knobkerries. The gifts were intended to facilitate the couple's start of married life.

The next morning, the initiation tutors and selected members of both families would meet the couple at the groom's place to conclude their teaching (*ukusulula ifiteta*). This took almost a full day as lessons given earlier during the wedding procedure were revised. Both female and male tutors participated by going over all the instruction given from the Chisungu initiation onward. Tutors took turns teaching and to accentuate mutuality in marriage, bride and groom each had to repeat their every word. Addressing the groom, tutors would sing:

Icikulu mwaume mu nganda	The man is the head of the house
Efyo twaumfwa	That is what we have been told
Na banakashi abapikula cisumpe	Women make the pinnacle also.

They meant to say that a husband need not be too preoccupied with family headship. While he is the head of the household, he should know that his wife is leader of the family and leader in marriage rituals. In other words, respect for one another is important.

They would also sing:

Icipuna	Stool
Bamuteka pa kapuna	He has made her sit on the stool
Ni Lesa wamusansabike	It is God who exalted her

According to this song, women can be leaders because God put them in charge of certain aspects of marriage and of life in general. There should be mutual respect and love in marriage.[17] At this point, the actual wedding ceremony came to an end.

6.3.1. 5 Rituals to undo taboos governing the son-in-law

The marriage process would be continued later with a ritual to undo taboos to which a son-in-law was subjected (*ukwingisha shifyala*). The ritual removed for example a taboo on the groom's movements in the in-law's house and from now on he was allowed to physically enter the house and the bedroom of his parents-in-law. This ceremony could take place only after the couple had two or more children. No such ceremony was held for a son-in-law who had no children. The ritual showed appreciation for the son-in-law's contribution to the success of the marriage. Only a deserving son-in-law would be honoured in this way. He was now also free to take his wife to his own family from time to time. As a mark of appreciation (*umuchinshi*) the son-in-law gave gifts to his parents-in-law.This ritual was also punctuated by singing. When the groom and his family entered the in-law's house, the wife's relatives sung:

Mwaingilamo!	You have entered!
Muganda yacipungu lisheni amapi.	In the house of an eagle clap your hands.
Mwaingilamo!	You have entered!
Muganda yacipungu lisheni amapi.	In the house of an eagle clap your hands.

They were reminding him that he now entered the house of the in-laws that, thus far, he couldn't enter. As a way of confirming that the taboo had been undone, the son-in-law was allowed to inspect every room in the house while those present sang:

Nshimba konkola,	Genet inspect,
Konkola.	Inspect.
Konkola noomu,	Inspect here,
Konkola.	Inspect.
Konkola noomu,	Inspect here,
Konkola.	Inspect.

In the future, if his in-laws were unwell, or in case of an emergency, he would be free to enter their bedroom and help them.

If the son-in-law felt that his in-laws did not appreciate him, he would sing:

Itumba lilela	The drum is sounding
Kanshi kumako balenjeba fimbi.	But the in-laws are telling me something else
Bantulile ngoma	They have torn my drum
Shicasulwa nabanyina fyala	Me who is not respected by the mother in-law

If he had demonstrated the power of fecundity and become known for sexual prowess (nga mwaume), his wife's grandmother would sing:

Chula ula wamya	Frog you are fascinating
Chula ula wamya	Frog you are fascinating
Pakufukafuka ye pabwendo bobe	When dancing at your hole
Chula ula wamya	Frog you are fascinating

The ritual reflected that the groom had been fully accepted by his wife's family and the marriage rites were completed.

6.4 CONCLUSION

Chapter six discusses the purpose, form, and practice of marriage initiation rites among the Bemba people of Zambia. Marriage in pre-colonial Bemba society was seen as the union of a man and a woman for life. It signified the bringing together of the families of the bride and groom. It was a social event and involved the support of the entire community. As an institution marriage mirrored the fabric of society. The teaching and the rituals performed provided a moral framework or a code of conduct for the couple and the wider society. The lessons emphasized hygiene, hospitality, the need to take care of one's family, the social and religious roles of a woman, maximising satisfaction during sexual intercourse, sticking to one sexual partner and spacing the arrival of babies. A closer look at the present form and practices of wedding ceremonies in Bemba communities reveals continuities as well as discontinuities in the various practices.

CHAPTER SEVEN

GENDERED CULTURAL VALUES OF MARRIAGE AND CHISUNGU INITIATION RITES

7.1 INTRODUCTION

Initiation rites involve the construction and definition of gender roles and identities. The present chapter is concerned with the gendered cultural values of indigenous marriage and Chisungu initiation rites. Details of the symbolic meaning of rites and an interpretation of some initiation songs and sacred emblems are provided. The teachings offered during the marriage and Chisungu initiation ceremonies represent social, political, religious, and moral meanings.[1] Given that gender roles and identities as constructed during initiation can be either life-giving or life-denying to women, it is necessary to examine the gendered values of marriage and initiation rites.

7.2 GENDERED CULTURAL VALUES

There is a tension between Christianity and indigenous African culture. Kanyoro shows that Christian women in Africa live as it were in two worlds with an allegiance to both African culture and Christianity.[2] This is certainly true of women in Bemba society. In pre-colonial, traditional, matrilineal, Bemba communities women were the head of their home. A married woman was in charge of all religious affairs and would lead prayers at the shrine (*imfuba*). Furthermore, women's leadership roles were demonstrated and emphasized during the Chisungu initiation rites.[3]

The gendered values and elements of the traditional culture survive today in indigenous marriage and Chisungu initiation rites when a woman is taught about her original role and status in society. The initiate gets information about the clan's origin and destiny, the community's notion of God and her own sacred leadership position as a married Bemba woman. The rites affirm and demonstrate women's authority in society.

On the second day of Chisungu initiation, the initiate is taken into the bush for libation and rituals. Beer is poured on the mufungo tree and the initiate prays after throwing white beads to the east and the west saying: *Twabusha impanga, mwe mipashi yesu mu twiminineko* ("We have cleared the forest. Spirits of our grandparents be with us"). The initiate next has to take the beads hanging over branches using her mouth. The east signifies future, light, and happiness. The west (*Kola*) is the past and the home of the ancestors.[4] The beads are a symbol of marriage and purity.[5] Taking them with the mouth implies a warning against premarital and extramarital sex which is believed to cause a 'slimming' illness (*ukulepa iminwe*).

The initiate is made aware of the presence of the mother-father God (*Lesa*). Kaunda points out that, connected to the roles of women, is the belief in a mother-father God (*Mayo/Tata Lesa*).[6] While a Bemba God is believed to be both feminine and masculine as in *Mayo Tata Lesa*, during Chisungu initiation it is usually the feminine image of God that is invoked, as in *Lesa nankoko uwafukatila abana* which means "God who is caring like the mother hen."[7]

It is clear from the above that God is perceived by Bemba people as having both feminine and masculine identities. Leaders as well are expected to possess feminine virtues in addition to masculine attributes. What this means for Christianity and its influence on Bemba women needs further interrogation. Poewe points out that in Bemba society leaders are seen as reaching perfection when they acquire characteristics of the opposite sex.[8] Women tutors of initiation rites are considered to be ritual males. The names of shrines are seen as feminine. God can only be reached by imitating the feminine attributes. Hence, there appear to be values in Bemba culture that if reclaimed for the sake of empowering women would allow for a critique of patriarchy from within.

Male power in society and the violence against women that may accompany it, is in religious contexts often reinforced by an exclusive use of male terms in reference to God.[9] Reclaiming the "mother-father image" of God may promote mutual respect between men and women and, therefore, empower women.

The initiate is taught that the three annual seasons symbolize male and female. The cold and dry season (May to July) is harvesting time and symbolizes the feminine. The hot season (September to November) stands for the masculine while the rainy season unites the two other seasons symbolizing the perfect union of man and woman as well as the divine gift of fecundity bestowed on their meeting in the rainy season. The earth is the symbol of the womb that waits patiently for the divine rains so as to become fertile. The sun stands for the divine, and the morning rays of the sun symbolize the male power of fecundity.

Access to God is, therefore, only possible through the marriage union of husband and wife.[10] It is believed that access to God for the well-being of the community can only be realized through sexual intercourse in marriage with a woman who should be approached with patience and reverence.

A menstruating woman is considered to be in the cold season. She is therefore not allowed to cook, add salt to food, and have sexual intercourse. It is thought that salt weakens the body and the husband or another family member is expected to do the cooking at this time. The woman wears red beads to indicate to her husband that she is having her period.[11] This taboo is aimed at giving the woman time to rest. The idea that she is unclean because of the menstrual blood has been condemned by African women theologians. Oduyoye argues that an association of certain elements of African religio-culture that portray menstrual blood as dangerous with views presented in the Old Testament have resulted in Zambian women becoming disempowered and deprived of leadership roles in church and society.[12]

The initiate is taught about the important use of beads (ubulungu/chisasa). The stringing of beads symbolises parenthood and purity in marriage. The saying, Lesa bulungu, tapita paka fundo ("God is like beads through which no knot can pass"), means that sexual purity must be maintained in marriage. Extra-marital relations are disapproved of. Also, the bridegroom is advised on the importance of purity as in the saying, sunga umukoshi ubulungu tabwayafya ("Look after your neck properly; it is easy to find beads"), meaning that faithfulness of husband and wife results in God blessing them with children.[13] This emphasis on fidelity and purity in marriage arises from the belief that the 'mother-father' God can only be approached through marital sexual relations. For this reason marriage is highly valued and celibacy is not admired.[14]

7.3 INDIGENOUS ROLES OF WOMEN

Given that there are continuities and discontinuities in the performance of marriage and Chisungu initiation rites in the pre-colonial era and today, it is important to evaluate the roles of women as these were passed on from one generation to another during rites in pre-colonial times and to consider the lessons given to initiates about their religious and social tasks.

The main function of the woman was to be *chibinda wa ng'anda* (owner of the home). Hinfelaar is of the view that this was a religious qualification of women as enablers of the domestic cult. However, the role emphasized both religious and social leadership positions of women as owners and heads of the household.[15] *Chibinda* means 'owner' as in: *Lesa e chibinda wa myeo yesu* or "God is the owner of our lives." The marriage home was a symbol of the woman's womb. She was responsible for the well-being of the marriage and the husband had to approach her with respect in matters of sex.

As mentioned above, sexual intercourse within marriage was believed to have spiritual force, and if handled in the right manner, could be used for the benefit of the whole community. For this reason, chiefs performed special acts of intercourse for the sake of bringing blessings to the community and fertility to the land.[16] Sex was, therefore, considered sacred and had to be part of a committed married relationship.

Consequently, the initiate was taught to ensure that sex only took place in a faithful marriage. Any deviation was thought to affect both partners as well as their children. In a traditional Bemba society, the wife may refuse sexual intercourse if she is not convinced of her husband's faithfulness.[17] It is believed that a husband's extra-marital affairs could cause a pregnant wife to die (*inchila*). If a woman dies in pregnancy, her husband is severely punished.

Another belief is that extra-marital affairs conducted by a pregnant wife will cause her death immediately after giving birth (*incentu*). Hence, the crucial importance of fidelity is as in *wilasankanya umulopa* ("never mix conjugal blood") or *wilacila umukashi* ("don't step over your wife's spirit").[18] Adultery and fornication are severely punished. Incompatibility and ill-treatment of the wife would lead to the separation of the partners because in such circumstances the role of the wife as the owner of the house would be compromised.[19]

The second role of the woman was to initiate worship (*Kabumba wa mapepo*). *Kabumba* means 'creator' as in *Lesa Kabumba* (God the creator). The Bemba believe that women, during the initiation ceremony and through the use of marriage emblems (*imbusa*), ensure that God is present. Hinfelaar observes that this belief points to the religious role of women.[20] It also was her responsibility to take offerings to the family shrine and to lead prayers to God for the well-being of the family. Similarly, women were in charge of territorial shrines where they conducted prayers to God through the medium of the ancestors for the well-being of the whole community. It is therefore, evident that the function of indigenous Chisungu initiation rites went well beyond simply giving sexual education.

Richards mentions that if lessons on sex and motherhood were more emphasized than instruction on prayers to the ancestors and religious leadership of women, this was due to the introduction of Christianity and western civilisation.[21] It is worth noting that Christianity reinforced by colonial authorities considered worship of the ancestors as idolatry. In addition, the missionaries and the colonial powers did not recognize women as religious leaders, and priests were predominantly male. Christianity and colonialism have, therefore, disempowered women by detracting from their religious leadership roles, leading to the gradual disappearance of this component in Chisungu initiation rites.

A third aspect of the initiation rites that women learned about was concerning the Chisungu as *nachimbusa wa chisungu* (mother of the marriage, or sacred emblems). The first menstruation (*ukuwa ichisungu*) was cerebrated as a wondrous event whereby the young woman received God's gift of her sexuality. Hinfelaar argues that the title implied by *na chimbusa wa Chisungu* refers only to the role of the initiation tutor (*nachimbusa*).[22] However, during Chisungu initiation women are pointedly reminded of their role as mother of the sacred emblems in the community (*ifimbusa*).

The rituals clearly center on reminding women of the values of Bemba culture that safeguard their dignity and of the importance of passing on those values to the next generation. *Mbusa* means 'things to be handed down.' The 'things to be handed down' are values that must be preserved and passed on from generation to generation like the stringing of beads.

Richards describes an initiation tutor who "reckoned herself as of royal rank although she was only a member of a junior branch of a royal clan. She had an unusual personality, great organising power, and a sharp tongue."[23] Although her perception of the role of *nachimbusa* was coloured by western lenses, she recognized that *nachimbusa* did hold leadership positions in Bemba society. Given that lessons and the gendered values are delivered to the initiate through marriage or sacred emblems the following section discusses the major types of emblems and their meanings.

7.4 SACRED EMBLEMS

Four types of sacred emblems are used during the initiation ceremony. The first type of emblems consists of traditional food that is essential to the Bemba people such as millet, beans, groundnuts, pumpkin seeds, game meat, fish, and salt. Each kind of food has a meaning. Another group of emblems consists of fruit bearing trees such as *mufungo* and *musuku* trees. Each tree also has a meaning of its own and features in a song performed during the ceremony. The third type consists of pottery emblems, usually painted in white, red, and black. Emblems have their own names and songs.[24] A fourth kind of emblems consists in wall designs painted on the inside wall of the initiation house. Design patterns are known by specific names and have generally accepted meanings.

The interpretation of initiation songs and sacred emblems has evolved over time. This is due to the advent of Christianity and (post)modernity. That the understanding of elements of initiation rites grows and deepens over time becomes clear from Richard's account of the way in which an old initiation tutor interpreted the songs as compared to the approach of Paul Mushindo who was a minister at Lubwa mission of the Church of Scotland (now UCZ).[25] Nowadays, in urban areas where it is not possible to make pottery emblems, these are presented in the form of visual aids or wall designs.

Before the presentation and explanation of sacred emblems, the initiation tutor gives a marriage pot (*akalongo*) to the initiate. She is told to always remember to prepare 'love meals' called *akatemba cupo* ('love meal' or 'marriage holder') which husband and wife should eat in the bedroom. The love aspect is brought out in husband and wife feeding each other.[26] The special love meal aims to promote sharing and love in marriage.

7.4.1 EMBLEMS OF TRADITIONAL FOODS

After the presentation of the marriage pot, the initiate is presented with sacred emblems in the form of traditional foods. Lessons on traditional foods usually focus on good nutrition for the family. Women are also taught that certain foods such as groundnuts can boost the sex drive.

7.4.2 EMBLEMS OF FRUIT-BEARING TREES

The initiate is introduced to tree emblems such as *mufungo* and *mwenge* trees when she is taken into the bush. Tree emblems are fruit-bearing (female) trees that represent fertility and the sacredness of the woman and male trees that represent the groom.[27]

The women pour beer on the ground under the tree emblems. The making of beer is during initiation emphasized as an important duty of married women. It is this beer that motivates the ancestors to bless the occasion and the initiate. The role of beer conflicts with some Christian teaching that beer is evil. The church often admonishes women who are reported to have been drinking beer during an initiation or wedding ceremony.

After the beer has been poured out, the initiate is introduced to the *mulombwa* or *nakabumbu* (male trees) representing the bridegroom. The red bark fruit of the *mulombwa* tree represents the menstruation blood and warns of the danger of mixing marital blood through infidelity.

7.4.3 CLAY/POTTERY EMBLEMS

Among the different emblems made of clay are mortar and pestle. They symbolize the unity of soul and spirit between husband and wife through marital sex.[28] A second clay emblem represents a hoe, pointing to the industriousness of the woman. The hoe also is a symbol of the married woman as a cultivated garden through which no man but her husband is allowed to pass. A man is not expected to signal any sexual interest to a married woman.

The third emblem depicts a bracelet and a bead necklace. The bracelet represents the engagement price (*insalamu*) and stresses the husband's duty to provide for his wife. A man is considered as a fool if he is lazy and does not look after his wife. The necklace emphasizes the importance of the husband respecting the wife. If there is maltreatment or a lack of respect it is acceptable for a couple to separate.[29]

Another emblem shows a man with a big head and a big penis but without arms. He portrays a lazy man who is fond of finding fault with his wife and who doesn't appreciate her or respect her views. A fifth clay emblem is formed like a long snake (*yongolo*) and represents the man's penis. The emblem is a warning to the husband not to cheat in marriage. During initiation the groom is also told that it is out of bounds to have sex with a girl below the age of puberty or with a woman in the bush. The couple is encouraged to have sex whenever they want – but at home and not in the bush.[30] As sex is considered sacred it requires honourable behaviour. In addition, the bush is itself sacred because it is an abode of the ancestors and improper sex might defile it.

Another clay emblem shows a woman suckling her two children and carrying two other babies on her back (*choshi wa ngoma*). This emblem contains the obvious lesson that it is wise to let some time lapse between the births of children. The initiation tutor also stressed the importance of women refusing sexual intercourse until a baby had been weaned. The common Bemba practice is to let two to three years pass between pregnancies.[31]

At this stage of initiation, the initiate is presented with an emblem that depicts a woman carrying a basket on her head and another one carrying a basket in her hands. The basket is a symbol of marriage. The emblem signals the superior position of the woman in marriage and in her family. She is the head of the household and the pillar on which it rests.[32]

7.4.4 WALL DESIGNS

Lessons are also delivered using sacred emblems drawn on the walls of the initiation house or on some cloth. The interpretation of these particular emblems has also changed since pre-colonial times.

A first example of a wall emblem depicts a bean. The design represents the clitoris, the part of a woman's body that is responsible for sexual arousal. The initiate is taught to guide her husband to effect her sexual arousal. Richards ignorantly points out that in Bemba culture men are always expected to take the initiative in sex.[33] However, from the emblems it becomes clear that women are taught to let their wishes be known.

Another emblem shows a naked brother and sister standing flat against a wall. Richards suggests that this refers to some form of incest in Bemba indigenous culture.[34] However, the image is of brother-sister bonding and equality which is part of Bemba matrilineal culture and which prescribes that children belong to the mother and are the possible heirs of her brother.

An emblem of a standing man and woman with a stick between them and two animals resembling each other eating from one plate refers to the equality of husband and wife united as they are by sexual intercourse.[35]

A fourth emblem depicts a rectangular bed without blankets. It tells the woman to stay with her husband even if they are short on material possessions (*chipuba chobe*).[36] Divorce for materialistic reasons is not acceptable. The emblem also warns that no man should seduce a woman in the bush where there is no shelter.

On another emblem we see a naked woman with a big red vulva, signifying that women should have long genitals to satisfy their husbands.[37] Long genitals are a woman's pride and she should pull the labia and keep her vagina tight and dry.

An emblem showing hands and a razor reminds the couple of the need to clean each other after sex and to shave their armpits and private parts.[38] Richards writes, incorrectly, that there is no intimacy in Bemba marriage. But the cleaning of each other after sex is a clear indication of the closeness of marriage partners.

An emblem depicting a bird called *mung'omba* that sings early in the morning tells initiates to wake up in good time and ask their husbands for intercourse. Early in the morning is believed to be the best time to have sex.[39]

The wall emblem called *mushintililo* (mutual understanding), representing a target, is featured towards the end of initiation. The groom-to-be enters the initiation house with bow and arrow. The climax of this ritual is when he faces east and shoots an arrow into the target on the west wall of the house.[40] The emblem tells the couple that success in marriage and life depends on mutual understanding. If this ceremony is performed in the course of marriage proceedings, it is followed by the consummation of marriage. The bridegroom is referred to as an indomitable lion (*mundu*) or king in the initiation ceremony. He is lion and king because the initiation ritual is associated with the potency of a king (*ukukafya umushi*). The powers of the king are protected by the usual Bemba marriage taboos. The king is responsible for the fertility and well-being of his people and he depends on the knowledge of his wife in performing conjugal rituals.[41]

Fiedler notes that indigenous initiation rites have been criticized for the use of obscene language, sexually suggestive dance movements, and sexual demonstrations.[42] However, sex needs to be discussed openly to enable women to enjoy it freely and to negotiate for safe sexual practices. Given that each marriage emblem comes with its own interpretation an in-depth discussion of female and male sexual organs is necessary.

7.4.5 FEMALE SEXUAL ORGANS AS DEPICTED BY THE EMBLEMS

During marriage and Chisungu initiation rites tutors explain the female reproductive system to the initiates. The system contains the uterus which hosts the developing fetus, produces vaginal and uterine secretions, and allows sperm

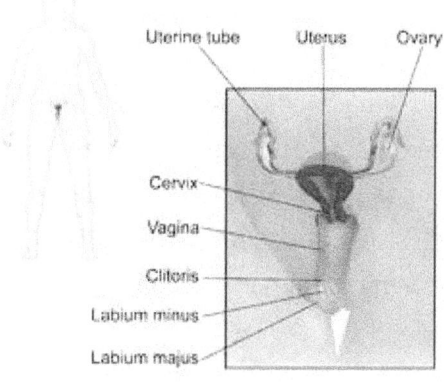

The Female Reproductive System

to pass through to the fallopian tubes, and the ovaries which produce the female's egg cells. These parts are internal. At the vulva the vagina meets the external organs, namely the labia, clitoris, and the urinary canal. The vagina is attached to the uterus by the cervix, while the uterus is attached to the ovaries by the fallopian tubes. At certain intervals the ovaries release an ovum which passes through the fallopian tubes into the uterus. If, in transit, it meets with sperm, a single sperm can enter and merge with the egg and fertilization takes place.[43]

In this process, the egg is not a passive but rather an active participant, as it releases certain molecules that guide the sperm and that allow the surfaces of egg and sperm to become attached. The egg now absorbs the sperm and fertilization begins. Fertilization usually occurs in the oviducts but can happen in the uterus itself. In that case, a zygote will divide itself over several generations of cells to form a blastocyst that penetrates into the uterus wall where it starts the processes of embryogenesis and morphogenesis. When it is sufficiently developed to survive outside the womb, the cervix dilates and contractions of the uterus propel the fetus through the birth canal, which is the vagina.[44]

7.4.5.1 Ova

Ova (*utubulungwa twabufyashi*) are larger than sperm and form by the time a female is born. Approximately every month, one ovum matures to be sent down the fallopian tube attached to the ovary in anticipation of fertilization. If it is not fertilized, the egg is flushed out of the female system through menstruation.

7.4.5.2 Vagina

The vagina (*inyo/ubwanakashi*) is a fibro-muscular tubular tract leading from the uterus to the exterior of the body. It is where semen from the male penis is deposited into a female's body at the climax of sexual intercourse which is called ejaculation. The vagina is the canal that runs from the cervix (the lower part of the uterus) to outside the body. It is also known as the birth canal.

7.4.5.3 Cervix

The cervix (*intendekelo yanshila yabwanakashi*) is the lower, narrow portion of the uterus where it joins the top end of the vagina. It is cylindrical or conical in shape and protrudes through the upper anterior vaginal wall. Approximately half its length is visible to the naked eye; the remainder lies above the vagina beyond view. The vagina has a thick outside layer and is where the fetus emerges during delivery. It is also named the neck of the uterus.

7.4.5.4 Uterus

The uterus or womb (*ichisa*) is the major female reproductive organ. It provides the developing embryo (weeks one to eight) and the fetus (week nine until delivery) with mechanical protection and nutritional support, while securing waste removal. In addition, the contractions performed by the muscular wall of the uterus are important and push the fetus out at the time of birth.

The uterus is a pear-shaped muscular organ. Its major function is to accept fertilized ovum that becomes implanted into the endometrium and derives nourishment from blood vessels which develop exclusively for this purpose. The fertilized ovum becomes an embryo, and thereafter, a fetus. If the egg does not get embedded in the uterus wall the female will menstruate.

7.4.5.5 Fallopian tubes

The fallopian tubes or oviducts (*inshila yatubulungwa twabufyashi*) are two tubes leading from the ovaries of a woman into the uterus. On maturity of an ovum, the follicle and the ovary's wall rupture, allowing the ovum to escape and enter the fallopian tube. There it travels toward the uterus, pushed along by movements of cilia on the inner lining of the tubes. This trip may take hours or days. If the ovum is fertilized while in the fallopian tube, it normally becomes implanted in the endometrium when it reaches the uterus. This signals the beginning of pregnancy.

7.4.5.6 Labia majora

The labia majora (*imishino/imilomo yabwanashi iyakunse*) are two folds of skin that extend from the front to the back of the vaginal opening. The outer surfaces of the folds have darker-coloured skin and stronger hairs while the inner folds are smoother. The labia majora join to form the cleft shape of the female genitals also known as the pudendal cleft or the cleft of Venus, after the Roman goddess of love.[45]

7.4.5.7 Labia minora

Between the labia majora are the labia minora (*imishino/imilomo yabwanakashi iyamukati*), two folds of skin extending downward from the clitoris around the vaginal opening. These labia vary in size from woman to woman. They are joined by a small fold of skin known as the "little fork." This can get torn in childbirth or during acts of sexual violence.

7.4.5.8 Clitoris

The clitoris (*soswe/chilemba*) is a crucial element for sexual arousal in most women. This small organ is located at the top of the vagina at the junction of the labia minora and it appears outside the folds of skin like a small pink button. During sexual stimulation, the clitoris functions much like a man's penis in that it becomes erect. This is because the shaft under the skin has erectile tissues which become congested with an increased blood flow when stimulated. The clitoris is very sensitive to stimulation and most women cannot achieve orgasm without direct stimulation of the clitoris.

7.4.5.9 Urethra

The urethra (*inshila ya misu*) is located between the vaginal opening and the frontal connection of the labia minora. It is the opening where urine gets expelled.

7.4.6 MALE SEXUAL ORGANS AS DEPICTED BY THE EMBLEMS

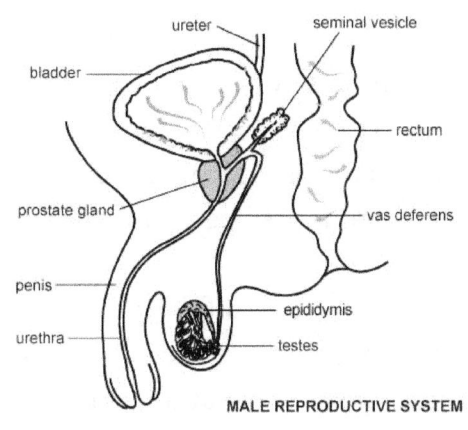

MALE REPRODUCTIVE SYSTEM

7.4.6.1 Penis

The penis (*ubukala*) is the male intromittent organ. It has a long shaft and an enlarged bulbous-shaped tip called the glans penis, which supports and is protected by the foreskin in uncircumcised males. When the male is sexually aroused, the penis becomes erect and ready for sexual activity. Erection occurs because sinuses within the erectile tissue of the penis become filled with blood. The arteries of the penis are dilated while the veins are compressed so that blood flows into the erectile cartilage under pressure.[46]

7.4.6.2 Scrotum

The scrotum (*amatole*) is a pouch-like structure that hangs behind the penis. It holds and protects the testicles. It also contains numerous nerves and blood vessels. In low temperatures, the Cremaster muscle contracts and pulls the scrotum closer to the body, while the Dartos muscle gives it a wrinkled appearance. When the temperature increases, the Cremaster and Dartos muscles relax to bring the scrotum down and away from the body thus removing the wrinkles. The scrotum is connected with the abdomen or pelvic cavity by the inguinal canal. The spermatic cord, consisting of the spermatic artery, vein, and nerve bound together with connective tissue passes through the inguinal canal into the testis.

7.4.6.3 Testes
The paired oval testes, also known as the male gonads (*infyo/intoyo*), hang in the scrotal sac. Usually the right testis hangs higher than the other by about 1 cm. They hang outside the body because the body temperature is too high for the production of sperm, which is made in the testes at a temperature about 3 °C below body temperature.

7.4.6.4 Epididymis
The epididymis (*imishipa ya mumatole*) is a whitish mass of tightly coiled tubes cupped against the testicles. It acts as an area of maturation and storage for sperm before they pass into the vas deferens that carries it to the ampullary gland and prostatic ducts.

7.4.6.5 Vas deferens
Joined to the epididymis is the vas deferens (*imishipa ya malume*) which is a thick walled tube that transports sperm from the epididymis up to the prostate gland. The part of the vas deferens that lies above the testis can be felt through the loose part of the scrotum. The vas deferens empties into the ejaculatory duct that passes through the prostate gland to merge with the urethra.

7.4.6.6 Accessory glands

Three accessory glands (*insande sande shabwaume*) provide fluids that lubricate the duct system and nourish the sperm cells. They are the seminal vesicles, the prostate gland, and the bulbourethral glands.

7.4.6.7 Urethra

The urethra (*inshila ya misu*) is the tube through which urine passes from the bladder via the penis to the body's exterior. It is also the tube through which semen is ejaculated.

7.4.7 THE GIZZARD AS DEPICTED BY THE EMBLEMS

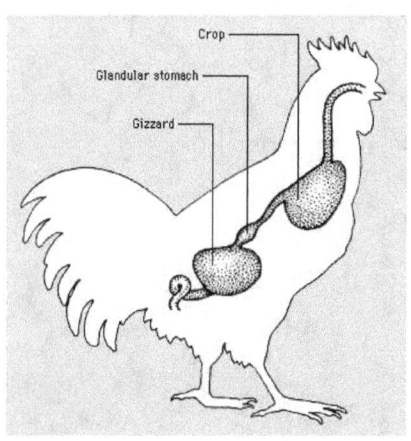

The gizzard, also referred to as the *ventriculus* or the gastric mill, is an organ found in the digestive tract of birds.[48] It is a kind of specialized stomach with thick muscular walls. It serves to grind food, often aided by particles of stone or grit. The Bemba people of Zambia consider the chicken's gizzard as symbolically important, and it has ritual significance during marriage and female initiation rites.

As a marriage emblem, the gizzard symbolizes the scrotum in the male reproductive organs. The grit present on the inside of the gizzard stands for the sperm. During marriage and female initiation rites women are taught that only their husbands should eat the gizzard. When visitors come and a chicken is killed, the gizzard is, as a token of hospitality, offered to the visitors. If there is no gizzard, it signals that the chicken was not killed especially for the visitors, implying a lack of hospitality and respect.

7.5 THE PLATEAU OF LOVE

During marriage initiation rites the couple is taught about all those parts of the body that, when touched, lead to sexual arousal.[49] These include:

Body openings such as eyes, nose, mouth, and ears.

where hair ends	neck	abdomen
buttocks	thighs	breasts
clitoris	labia minora and labia majora	
vagina	urethra	anus

The initiation lessons emphasised that a man is easily sexually aroused while a woman takes longer. She also takes longer to reach resolution after orgasm.[50]

THE PLATEAU

Arousal/excitement stage

MAN: Penis erection, scrotum swells, blood flows, blood pressure increases, pulse rate increases, sweating.

WOMAN: Nipples swell, breasts swell, flushing of blood, clitoris swells, excretion of mucus in the vagina, labia swell.

Plateau stage
      MAN: Penis becomes strong, scrotum swells, pleasure starts.
      WOMAN: Breasts and nipples become strong, vagina contracts, uterus, cervix and muscles contract, buttocks contract.

Orgasm stage
      MAN: Penis pumps, ejaculation, buttocks contract, pleasure.
      WOMAN: Contraction of muscles around vagina (5-12 times), uterus, cervix and muscles contract, buttocks contract, pleasure.

Resolution stage
      MAN: Penis and scrotum become soft, blood pressure falls.
      WOMAN: Vagina, labia and muscles relax, blood pressure falls.

Songs play an important role in the delivery of lessons on sexuality. Given that each sacred/marriage emblem comes with its own song(s) and interpretations, an in-depth discussion of some initiation songs is relevant to the purpose of this book.

7.6 INITIATION SONGS IN COLONIAL AND POST-COLONIAL TIMES

7.6.1 FIRST DAY
On the first day of her initiation, the initiate is led crawling into the initiation house, covered with a blanket while women are singing:

Twingile shani?	How shall we go in?
Twingile mwi pempe;	Let us go into the dark tunnel;
Twingile nga Kolwe	Let us go in like monkeys.

The song announces the initiate's transition from childhood to adulthood. She has to be in seclusion which is a dark and difficult place before she can expect to acquire wisdom.[51] She is subjected to physical pain. Her thighs will be pinched especially if she is known to the community as being stubborn.

The second song goes:

Wakula nomba wansanga	You are now grown up like me
We mwengele wandi	My pine tree.
Wakula nomba wansanga	You are now grown up like me
We mwengele wandi	My pine tree.

The song shows the change in the status of the initiate. As an adult woman she is from now on expected to behave in a socially acceptable manner. In the next song the women sing:

Ulelolesha Intanda ubushiku	You gaze at the stars at night
Ulantuka ukukashika	You insult me obscenely

The song tells the initiate that, however bad a man insults his wife and quarrels with her, she should not answer back. It also warns the husband not to insult the wife by referring to her menstrual blood.

7.6.2 THE SECOND DAY

On the second day in the bush, the initiate is made to climb the musuku tree with her legs up while women sing:

Fulwe tanina	The tortoise does not climb
Lelo anina ku mukolobondo	But today it is climbing the tree

In other words, a woman must learn to do the impossible. She may not be a man, but she must take over his tasks if need be.[52]

The second song is accompanied by a dance referring to sex. The initiate dances with legs wide open, holding her dress high up while women sing:

| Butanda ndeka | Reed mart let me go |
| Nakumbwa inama kwisano | I have admired fresh meat at the palace |

The words indicate that a married woman has every right to enjoy sex. If her husband is impotent or does not satisfy her, she is free to get someone from within the family to help out sexually as long as it is done discreetly.[53]

At night they sing:

Kasusu tole nda	Little bat pick the louse,
Leka ichungulo cise	Wait for the evening to come
Tubike muleya pambali	We will put amorous play aside

This song represents a woman who goes out to hunt for lovers at night in the dark. It teaches the initiate to avoid promiscuity. A woman should also not expose her body to seduce a man she does not know.

7.6.3 THE THIRD DAY

Most of the songs sung at night on the third day address both the initiate and her bridegroom. When he arrives with bow and arrow, women sing:

Iseni mutambe	Come and see!
Tuchitwale uko bachibashile	Let us take her to where she was made
Napelwa no mulume wankalamu	I have been given to my lion
Iseni mutambe	Come and see

The song announces that the initiate is ready for the occupations of married life. The women present her to her husband who is as strong as a lion.[54] The song reduces the responsibilities of the married woman to only one, namely, satisfying her husband.

The second song is addressed to the bridegroom.

| Nalonsha inama yandi | I have tracked my game; |
| Tabula mwine walasa | I have shot one |

Initiate and groom are told that a man should be potent enough to satisfy his wife during sexual intercourse.

The third song is addressed to the bridegroom.

Icikulu mwaume mu nganda	The man is the head of the house
Efyo twaumfwa	That is what we have been told
Na banakashi abapikula cisumpe	Women make the pinnacle also.

The bridegroom is made to understand that man and woman can both be head of the household. He should realise that while he is expected to solve problems at home, a marriage will never prosper without the wisdom of the wife. The marriage tutor warns the bridegroom: Umupini ukulangile umwanakashi libwelelo ("Always pay attention to your wife's advice; if you don't, you will live to regret it.")

The fourth song addresses the initiate:

Mayo akabambe kambaba munda
    Mother, a maggot is itching in my stomach
Mayo akabambe kanshi kalababa?
    Mother, so a maggot itches?

This song tells the initiate that, if her husband infects her with a sexually transmitted illness (STI), she should not hide the fact but share it with someone she trusts.[55] This also implies that husbands have to respect their wives and not take them for granted. The fifth song tells the initiate:

Chibale chibale Chibale Chibale
Kasambe umulume Go and wash your husband
We chinangwa we You uninitiated creature

As we have seen, she has to clean her husband after sexual intercourse. She must also ensure that his pubic hair is cut. If a married man dies with long pubic hair the widow gets mistreated by his relatives.[56] Several songs teach about hygiene, hospitality, and maintaining good relations with in-laws.

Other songs performed during marriage and Chisungu initiation rites, as well as marriage emblems used for teaching, stress the equality and the leadership roles of women. La Fontaine notes that the emphasis on the subordination of wife to husband does not seem consistent with the observed reality of women's lives in traditional Bemba culture as they clearly had freedom of choice.[57] Rasing adds that Bemba women were among the neighbouring peoples admired for their industry and independence. Bemba royal women played a role in political and religious life and were in charge of ancestral shrines. Also a common woman commanded respect as the mother of her brother's heir. The current overwhelming preoccupation with patriarchy in marriage and in Chisungu initiation rites is, therefore, I would argue, due to external factors such as the influence of Christianity and western civilisation and their interaction with patriarchal African non-Bemba cultures.

7.7 CONCLUSION

Chapter seven focuses on the gendered cultural values of marriage and Chisungu initiation rites. It explains the symbolical meanings of the rites, the sacred emblems, and the initiation songs. The chapter discusses the indigenous gendered roles of Bemba women and the cultural values relevant to their position in society. While there are, indeed, teachings that promote the subordination of women to men, the rites also expose values that promote mutuality and the traditional leadership roles of women. Because both positive and negative elements feature in marriage and Chisungu initiation rites, the negative aspects have to be corrected and the positive ones reclaimed. Phiri argues that initiation rites are a valuable tool for transmitting the mysteries of life to the next generation. She underscores the importance of being aware of the shortfalls in initiation rites while upholding those values that can empower both men and women. It may, therefore, well prove extremely worthwhile to retrieve the positive values of marriage and Chisungu initiation rites to promote egalitarianism.

CHAPTER EIGHT

RETRIEVING GENDERED CULTURAL VALUES OF MARRIAGE AND CHISUNGU INITIATION RITES

8.1 INTRODUCTION

Marriage and female initiation rites remain socially and culturally approved sources of information about matters of sex and the role of women in Africa.[1] The contributions made by marriage and Chisungu initiation rites to sex education and to issues concerning the role and status of men and women in Zambia is, therefore, critical in the response to social challenges such as gender based violence, the HIV pandemic, poverty, and climate change. This chapter demonstrates how gendered cultural values of indigenous marriage and Chisungu initiation rites can be retrieved and empower women who often find themselves restricted to a life in the margins of society. Given that the rites have both positive and negative aspects when it comes to gender equity, chapter eight will propose specific elements and practices that should be revised or removed and define those elements of which the retrieval would support the empowerment of women and promote equality.

8.2 NEGATIVE ASPECTS OF INITIATION RITES

An African initiation rite that has not been abandoned under the influence of Christianity and western civilisation must be based on a fundamental belief as Richards asserts.[2] Among such enduring rituals are Bemba marriage and Chisungu initiation. In view of the changes in contemporary society and the advent of social challenges such as climate change, the increase in cervical cancer and the HIV and AIDS pandemic, I would argue that these rites need to be revised so as to be life-giving to both men and women.

8.2.1 DEMYTHOLOGIZING SEX AND MENSTRUAL BLOOD

There are many perceptions of sex and menstrual blood in Bemba culture that need to be demythologised.[3] As earlier mentioned, traditional Bemba people believe that women and men who violate sex taboos will end up with a disease. Also, sex with a breastfeeding mother is thought to result in the baby suffering from chronic coughing. Abstinence during breastfeeding is used as a method for family planning based on the misconception that, as long as a woman is breastfeeding, she cannot fall pregnant. Such abstinence sometimes results in husbands having extra-marital affairs while waiting for the wife to wean their baby. This increases the vulnerability of the couple to sexually transmitted illnesses (STIs).

Myths and taboos concerning sex that are taught during initiation rites have a bearing on people's perception of the use of condoms. The resistance to condom use in Zambia is largely attributable to traditional African views on sex, how it should be performed and what its functions are. In traditional Zambian culture, sex is mainly linked to procreation, implying that it requires penetrative coitus involving the discharge of semen into a woman.[4] The implication is that any physical barrier is considered immoral. It is this view and not the perceived unreliability of condoms or fear to promote immorality which is responsible for the resistance to condom use in Zambian society.

In the Chisungu initiation rites, the process of menstruation is presented as dangerous and polluting.[5] Generally, in African culture, menstrual blood is believed to cause bad luck, contamination, and death. Women are perceived as possessing dangerous powers during menstruation. The loss of blood is thought to weaken the teaching of a religious functionary or even render it useless.[6] It is clear that menstruation taboos contribute to viewing women and their bodies as sources of pollution. This perception is highly problematic. Oduyoye is correct in arguing that the emphasis on sex taboos links women to evil and makes men innocent victims of sexuality.[7]

Other beliefs are that premarital and extra-marital sex causes bad luck, contamination, and death. According to Oduyoye, the stress on purity of sexual behaviour shows that African people feel uneasy about human sexuality.[8] It is this unease that prevents parents in African cultures from openly discussing matters of sex with their children. However, there is a need for such openness in respect to matters of sex. Kurian shows that "sexuality needs to be recognised as one of the many precious gifts from God.[9] It enables us to lead full and responsible lives including a satisfying sex life within a relationship." Demythologizing sex and looking at it as a gift from God may also help to empower women in the context of STIs.

Given that the initiation ceremony is a major cultural source of information about sexuality, men and women should both receive the same teachings to ensure mutuality and equality in marriage. Research supports the view that too much emphasis on the submissiveness of women to men and on their duty to satisfy men sexually, as is the case in Bemba culture, accounts for the weak position of women when it comes to negotiating for safe sex. It also makes women accept dry sex to please their men;[10] hence, a decision by tutors of marriage and Chisungu initiation rites to include lessons addressed to brides and may well promote mutuality and give women more power to protect their health. Research clearly indicates that HIV prevalence is high in countries where women have low status and little say over what kind of sexual practice they wish to engage in.[11]

In this context, marriage and Chisungu initiation rites could become a useful resource for promoting mutuality in marriage provided that bride and groom both receive the relevant instruction. Designing a pre-marital sex education programme for men and women to make sure that their married life is based on mutuality in decision making, and also including sex education, is ultimately empowering not only for women but also for men.

The issue of menstruation has caused agony for many African women. In Bemba culture, the wife communicates with the husband on matters concerning menstruation through wearing coloured beads. [12] Red beads mean she is menstruating; white beads indicate her period is over and sex can be resumed. Moyo argues that the use of beads gives women a certain degree of power as it leaves the decision when to stop and when to resume sexual relations in their hands.[13]

While there is some truth in this, it is more empowering for a woman to openly communicate with, and get respect from, her husband. Indigenous marriage and Chisungu initiation rites encourage a woman to freely exercise control over matters of sex. She is taught to initiate or refuse sex as she sees appropriate.[14] It might strengthen the woman's position if this was emphasized in tuition given to both women and men during the initiation ceremony. It would be life-giving to encourage open discussion about sex, not only between husband and wife, but also between parents and children. The role of initiation rites as channels of sex education and issues concerning the status of a woman in Zambian society might well prove crucial for the prevention of STIs.

8.2.2. DEMYTHOLOGIZING MARRIAGE

Marriage itself is in need of being stripped of myths in contemporary African societies.[15] The myths around marriage and related to sex have rendered African women highly vulnerable to STIs. Among Bemba people, marriage is considered as promoting the well-being of everyone involved. Celibacy is not encouraged. Impotence and barrenness are sufficient reasons for divorce or polygamy.[16] Married couples are expected to have sexual intercourse as often as possible, allowing for taboo periods such as menstruation or during the funeral of a relative. Procreation is important to ensure the continuation of the clan. A woman who dies without having given birth to a child is buried with a maize cob or small piece of charcoal inserted in the anus so that the spirit of barrenness does not come back to interfere with the living.[17]

While procreation may be one purpose of marriage, too much emphasis on fertility is problematic. Gnanadason states that in African culture a woman is conditioned from childhood onward to see marriage as her only purpose in life.[18] African culture prepares a woman for marriage, for society, and for her husband. In fact, the purpose of marriage has been limited to procreation. A strong focus on procreation in marriage and Chisungu initiation rites causes great unhappiness for unmarried and barren women who become alienated in, and are marginalized by, society. The problem of myths surrounding marriage and procreation goes beyond initiation circles to include the church. Oduyoye points out that many Christian church members follow the traditions upheld by African culture, namely, that a woman is not truly human if she hasn't given life to a child.[19] This reduces the status of women, and as Masenya observes, it makes women more vulnerable to STIs given that their husbands and society treat them as their property, preventing them from negotiating for protected sex.[20]

In Bemba culture, a man has to demonstrate his ability to produce children in marriage before he may approach the ancestors.[21] It becomes problematic where the wife is unable to bear a child and it leads some men to take a second wife or to have multiple sexual partners in pursuit of offspring. Furthermore, an unmarried adult woman is expected to be promiscuous and available for the pleasure of men. As a result, these women are often abused by men. In view of all these negative points, it would be hugely preferable to look upon marriage as an institution based on love and mutual commitment, rather than as a place that is meaningful solely in relation to procreation.

8.2.3 INSPECTION FOR LABIA ELONGATION

The Chisungu initiation rites include an inspection of the initiates for labia elongation. There also are marriage emblems that propagate the elongation of the labia and the tightening of the vagina.[22] Labia elongation is done gradually before puberty. Among the Bemba people tightening of the vagina is achieved by using herbs that reduce vaginal fluids and increase friction during intercourse.[23] Both procedures are believed to lead to increased satisfaction during sexual intercourse. The extended labia are seen as a reason for pride in the matrilineal Bemba society.[24]

Writing about labia elongation among the Yao people in Malawi, Klaus Fiedler argues that the practice is immoral, evil, and designed to make women more desirable to men. The elongation results from manipulating the labia.[25] While it may be true that elongated labia increase sexual satisfaction, tightening of the vagina is problematic in the context of STIs and cervical cancer.

As indicated by research, dry sex puts women at increased risk of HIV infection due to small tears occurring in the vagina surface. Vagina tightening and labia elongation make unprotected sex more dangerous.[26] The tears in the vagina and the herbs used for tightening it also make women more vulnerable to cervical cancer. Unfortunately, the ability of women to exercise control over their sexual behaviour may be limited by their financial dependence on men and their subordinate position in society. As long as these women cannot demand safe sex, labia elongation and tightening of the vagina pose a potentially lethal threat to their health and even their survival.[27]

Again, the socialisation during initiation where women are inspected for labia elongation may strengthen the perception that the major duty of a married woman is to satisfy her husband sexually.[28] This practice reinforces patriarchy and its negative effects on the lives of women. There is no doubt that, given the dangers resulting from dry sex, the practice needs to be discarded. However, while there are many initiation teachings that increase the vulnerability of women to serious illness and unhappiness, there are other values and practices that can empower women.

8.3 PRACTICES AND VALUES TO BE RETRIEVED

La Fontaine observes that the positive values of Chisungu initiation rites are curiously neglected.[29] The rites include values of a social, political, economic, and religious nature that represent a critique of patriarchy from within and that, if reclaimed, can increase the power of women. In the following section these values are explored.

8.3.1 ECONOMIC EMPOWERMENT OF WOMEN

In a traditional Bemba community, women were economically independent. Touwen relates how among pre-colonial Bemba groups, the wife did provide food for the family through gardening.[30] The husband usually was the hunter and assisted the wife in farming. Her participation in the agricultural economy consolidated the wife's position as breadwinner of the family. The relationship between wife and husband was, therefore, based on equality, and their roles complemented each other.

Poewe notes that Bemba matrilineal ideology encouraged separate but parallel participation of men and women in the economic and political affairs of Bemba society.[31] The political and economic contributions of women were valued as being of great importance. If the result was equality between the sexes, this changed when Christianity and western civilisation introduced the concept of the husband being the head of the household. The husband became the breadwinner, and the wife had to do domestic duties and look after the children.

Given that in traditional Bemba society the husband lived with his wife's family and that the wife headed the household, assigning her to the private sphere considerably weakened her economic position and status in society.[32] Christianity and western civilisation thus have disempowered Bemba women by enhancing the position of her husband leaving her, in today's context, exposed to challenges such as poverty, climate change, and STIs.

Research indicates that HIV prevalence is high among women who have a low status in society. Poverty and economic disempowerment may force women to accept having unprotected sex to accommodate the husband on whom they and their children depend to earn a living.[33] A holistic response to the threat of STIs and other challenges faced by women will have to address gender inequalities and increase the economic empowerment of women. Hence, reclaiming those values of initiation rites that promote the economic independence of women could prove an important tool in the prevention of STIs.

8.3.2 LEADERSHIP ROLES OF WOMEN

In pre-colonial matrilineal Bemba society, the status of women was comparatively high. Their social, religious, and political roles were emphasized during the initiation ceremony. They held positions equal to those occupied by men.[34] Women fulfilled religious roles as initiators of worship and social roles as tutors of initiation, but while married, they functioned as heads of their households.

Marriage and Chisungu initiation rites focus on the wife's role as head of the household. Kaunda's research confirms that in pre-Christian Bemba society, the wife as head of the house[35] presided over all marital affairs. Mutuality was a central value, and establishing a kind of hierarchy in the relationship between husband and wife was not encouraged.

In addition, the wife was in charge of religious affairs. As mentioned earlier, in pre-Christian Bemba society, God was conceived of as *Mayo Tata* or 'mother-father God.' The missionaries modified the concept and replaced it with the Judeo-Christian masculine God.[36] As the Bemba God (*Lesa*) was understood in relation to equality between men and women, especially in marriage, the belief in the 'mother-father God' had empowered women to exercise leadership.[37] Women were in charge of the family and of territorial shrines.[38] At these shrines and during initiation women were in close contact with nature and Mother Earth. The sacred emblems created by women during the initiation ceremony ensured God's presence among his/her people. This created a web of relationships linking people, nature, and God.[39]

The concept of the 'mother-father' God was passed on from one generation to another during the marriage and Chisungu initiation rites. By banning initiation rites, the framework within which women kept religious values alive over generations, the missionaries technically eliminated the concept of the 'mother-father' God among the Bemba people.[40] The ban also reduced the intensive contact of women with nature. Women were disempowered and transformed "from priestess and matriarchs to menstruating vulnerable women."[41] Reuther points out that male monotheism has promoted patriarchal rule and its social hierarchy by empowering men, elevating them as head of their family and society, and relegating women to marginal positions.[42]

Retrieving the 'mother-father' concept of God may help establish equality between men and women, especially in marriage.[43] Research indicates that the use of patriarchal language and a patriarchal conceptualisation of God in religious contexts contribute to male violence against women in society.[44] Driven by the high prevalence of HIV among women in heterosexual marriages, religious leadership roles of women in indigenous marriage and Chisungu initiation should be revived as they may prove life-giving to women. In addition, they might inspire women to maintain a close and holistic relationship with nature and the mother earth, which is necessary for finding an adequate response to climate change and the current ecological crisis.

Women tutors also fulfilled the role of training young women and girls during initiation enabling them to function optimally in traditional Bemba society. Moyo's research underlines that in traditional African societies, the matrilineal family system would accord significant leadership roles to women as overseers of shrines and in educating younger women so that they would become acceptable members of society.[45] In view of the above considerations, reinventing the traditional Bemba perception of the woman's position and providing relevant lessons to men and women together could provide Zambian society with an extremely useful strategy for building a healthier society.

8.3.3 PROTEST AND TALKING BACK
Masaiti asserts that,

> Zambian cultures such as [that of the] Bemba maintain that women should be submissive and listen to their husbands. It is a cultural belief that women need not be educated as this may encourage the woman to rule over the husband in the house. This hinders women's abilities to negotiate safer sexual practices.[46]

While patriarchy and a low status of women in society no doubt contribute to women failing to negotiate for safer sexual practices, Masaiti's assertion seems to imply that there isn't any aspect of Bemba culture that could improve the position of women to such a degree that they can communicate as equals with men. I argue, on the contrary, that indigenous Chisungu initiation rites offer several values that may empower women to protest if the need arises and to talk back.[47]

La Fontaine makes us aware that female initiation rites often contain examples of sexual license and obscenity and a resulting mockery of men.[48] Such a tendency is present also in the Chisungu initiation ceremony, specifically in emblems that depict male genitals, explicitly referring to sexuality. The licentious behaviour of women during initiation is a reversal of the patriarchal construction of how a woman ought to behave. In a patriarchal African society, a woman has to be humble and submissive. But in initiation ceremonies, women may behave outrageously and shout obscenities. La Fontaine further notes that this reversal is not a manifestation of resentment against men, but instead, represents opposition to cultural values that subordinate women to men.[49]

We have seen that the indigenous Chisungu initiation rites contain elements addressed specifically to the initiate's future husband who is always part of the ritual. The climax of the initiation involves the presentation and explanation of the marriage emblems to both bride and groom. The groom is made to understand that although he is a man his wife is the head of the house and its supporting pillar. He is also told to always listen to his wife's advice. In her turn, the wife is told, in the presence of the groom, to protest if needed and to share with others if the husband should infect her with a sexually transmitted disease.[50] In addition, the marriage emblems and the beads give the wife the power to decide when and how to have sex.

The Lumpa movement of Alice Lenshina in Zambia resulted from a protest by Bemba women against the imposition of a patriarchal Christian religious system by Catholic and Presbyterian missionaries.[51] Women protested against the banning of initiation rites and the missionaries' decision not to give women major church responsibilities.

Given that in marriage and Chisungu initiation marriage emblems are used that teach the importance of equality of men and women as well as the right of wives to protest and talk back to their husbands, it is evident that the current dominance of patriarchy among the Bemba people has been fuelled by external factors as pointed out above. There is no doubt that in some African cultures—Bemba culture among them—women have resisted male domination; therefore, as Maluleke states, the call for equality of men and women by African women theologians is not new or foreign to the African context (as claimed by some male theologians).[52]

In view of the need to be in control of their lives and bodies, it would be life-giving to women if they were ensured of the freedom to protest, to talk back, and in short, to stand up for themselves, for example, to demand safe sexual practices. Haddad correctly observes that with the continuing onslaught of HIV, the cries of women become more and more desperate.[53] Phiri and Nadar add that culture has been used to keep women from speaking out and that the 'talking back' of women implies a protest against patriarchy and an attempt to reclaim their voices and speak on a basis of equality with men.[54]

8.3.4 VIRGINITY TESTING AND DELAYING THE SEXUAL DEBUT

Chisungu initiation rites include virginity inspection. Virginity testing has been a controversial issue in relation to HIV and AIDS. Its purpose is to promote virginity and to encourage the initiate to avoid pregnancy before marriage which is in most African cultures considered as an abomination.[55]Because virginity testing in most cases focuses on women makes the practice problematic in the context of STIs. Society generally tends to expect women more than men to be careful and preserve their virginity.[56] In the contemporary society, people have gradually stopped talking about virginity. There is an underlying assumption that promoting virginity or abstinence would be too unpopular and doomed to failure. Safe sex is promoted instead.[57] However, behaviour change still remains an important tool in the prevention of STIs.

Bruce argues that although virginity testing is performed by African women who view it as a symbol of their African identity, the practice fits in with a perception that the HIV and AIDS pandemic is a result of women being sexually out of control.[58] Virginity testing attempts to exercise some control over women's stance on sexuality. Bruce warns that the temptation is to use the HIV pandemic for the endorsement of patriarchal cultural practices.[59] In a similar vein, Gomes reasons that linking the moral behaviour of a woman with the myth of virginity is problematic.[60] When a woman's sexuality is seen mainly as a means to satisfy men, it becomes a tool to oppress women.

Contrary to Bruce's and Gomes' views, Phiri argues that virginity testing is a good indigenous resource for the empowerment of women in Africa.[61] She describes how virginity testing is practised by female Zulu traditional healers to holistically heal abused girls and women. Virginity inspection in Chisungu initiation is, therefore, potentially a value that ought to be reclaimed in the context of STIs, including HIV and AIDS. However, as Bruce warns, it has to be done on such grounds and in such a way that it does not turn women into objects for men's sexual satisfaction.[62]

Virginity inspection may be useful if it aims to encourage young women and girls to delay becoming sexually active. According to research, an early sex debut contributes to a high risk of HIV infection and a high number of school drop-outs. An early involvement in sexual activity puts young people at a heightened risk of contracting STIs and falling pregnant. Delaying the sexual debut reduces such risks.[63] In addition, young adolescents often lack relevant knowledge and are likely not to use condoms. Virginity testing may, therefore, be a good traditional value to retrieve and to include in initiation rites, along with information on STIs and general sex education geared towards encouraging young women and girls to delay the sexual debut.

8.3.5 FIDELITY AND MULTIPLE SEXUAL PARTNERS

Marriage and Chisungu initiation rites include the instructing of a couple to uphold fidelity in marriage and avoid extra-marital affairs. Marriage has to be based on mutual understanding and love of two people.[64] As earlier stated, polygamy and having multiple sexual partners was not encouraged in pre-colonial Bemba society. It was thought to cause death and to jeopardize the role of the wife as initiator of worship. The advent of HIV and AIDS has raised a number of issues concerning polygamy and multiple sexual concurrences (MSC).

Philippe Denis argues that "polygamy is not dangerous, from an AIDS point of view, if the man limits his sexual contacts to his wives and the wives have no sexual activity outside the marriage."[65] Given the high prevalence of HIV among women in sub-Saharan Africa, including societies where polygamy is practised, Denis' assertions are problematic. Masenya observes correctly that among men in many African cultures, the expectation is that women have a duty to provide them with casual sexual gratification;[66] hence, there is usually no question of faithfulness to wives in a polygamous arrangement.

Phiri writes that women in heterosexual marriages in Africa, be they monogamous or polygamous, are exposed to a high risk of contracting STIs. She notes that reviving traditions in some African cultures where, after a long absence, a man is not allowed to have sex with his wife until it is certain that he has no sexually transmitted illness, may be life-giving to women. Similarly, reclaiming the value of marriage and Chisungu rites where the wife is in control of matters of sex and has the power to refuse sex if she has doubts about her husband's faithfulness, may safeguard women's health in the context of STIs. As mentioned above, during marriage initiation the couple was given a pot which they were not allowed to touch if one of them had committed adultery. Traditional beliefs holding that men are supposed to have multiple sexual partners (*ubuchende bwamwaume tabonaula inganda,* meaning "man's adultery does not affect marriage"), need to be opposed and broken. The HIV and AIDS pandemic challenges traditional and cultural views that men are ordained by God to have multiple sexual partners as a sign of masculinity. Women have to be given power in marriage to negotiate for safe sex practices. It is life-giving for a married couple to regularly test for STIs. If a husband has been away for a long time, the wife should be allowed to refuse sex until both have been tested for infectious diseases.

8.4 CONCLUSION

Chapter eight discusses parts of marriage and Chisungu initiation rites that, in a modern context, are harmful or on the contrary, may be life-giving. Practices such as vaginal tightening, inspection for labia elongation, taboos relating to sex and menstrual blood as well as myths about marriage that enhance the subordinate position of women in marriage and society, may, in view of health risks, be harmful and need to be revised or discarded. On the other hand, values and practices such as economic empowerment of women, reviving their traditional leadership roles, and their right to protest and talk back to their husbands, virginity inspection leading to delayed sexual activity and giving women power to negotiate for safe sex practices are life-giving and need to be retrieved. These values critique patriarchy from within and empower women. Because tutors of initiation rites are traditional teachers, it is vital that they possess adequate and correct information about STIs. This will equip them to warn against the health risks inherent in certain practices. Given that a gendered analysis of marriage and Chisungu initiation shows that the rites contain resources that can empower women to reclaim social, economic, religious, and marital leadership roles, chapter nine evaluates the importance of inculturating those resources for the purpose of promoting equality between men and women.

CHAPTER NINE

INCULTURATION OF INDIGENOUS MARRIAGE AND FEMALE CHISUNGU INITIATION RITES

9.1 INTRODUCTION

The question of inculturating marriage and female initiation rites has received much attention from African women theologians in the last two decades. Some of these condemn what they consider to be dehumanizing elements of marriage and female initiation rites, while others call for the Christianization of those values in the rites that are life-giving to women.[1] Specific values of female initiation rites have been inculturated, for example, in Malawi, but little effort in this direction has been made in other countries like Zambia, particularly in the Protestant churches, among them the UCZ.[2] Members of mothers' guilds have challenged the UCZ to embark on an inculturation process of indigenous Chisungu initiation. They argue that the rites may help to empower women in the context of HIV and AIDS.[3] The present chapter assesses the importance of inculturating the values of indigenous Chisungu initiation rites in Zambia.

9.2 INCULTURATION AS A THEOLOGICAL CONCEPT

The encounter between Christianity and African culture has presented African women with a dilemma. While some traditional African practices seem to be compatible with Christianity, others are not.[4] In response to western ways of doing theology, African theologians have started an inculturation project. The initial motive for the project was to Africanize Christianity by affirming African culture as a basis for doing theology.[5]

Martey notes that, when referring to Africanization or inculturation,[6] theologians make interchangeable use of the terms adaptation, incarnation, and indigenisation. Onsei-Bonsu stipulates that inculturation is different from the social science concepts of acculturation and enculturation.[7] He contends that acculturation is the encounter between two or more cultures, whereas, enculturation refers to the process of learning about a new cultural tradition through a process of socialisation.[8] According to Onsei-Bonsu,

> inculturation involves not only the process of introducing elements from the indigenous culture into Christianity, making use of thought-forms and concepts pertaining to the given culture; it also involves Christianising the indigenous culture, injecting it with Christian values, thereby transforming and reshaping it to produce a new creation.[9]

Inculturation is, therefore, the intimate transformation of positive cultural values through their integration into Christianity and the inserting of positive values of Christianity into a particular culture. In the context of the present author's argument, the process of inculturation involves a dialogue between the Gospel and the local African culture. A creative assimilation process takes place that begins with African culture of which it interprets those aspects that could enrich Christianity. In this way, Christianity is made to establish roots in African culture.[10] While affirming the need to reclaim values of traditional culture through a theology of inculturation, African women theologians are of the view that inculturation in itself is not sufficient unless the cultures, or the reclaimed values thereof, are life-giving to women.[11]

The critical question, however, is whether a process of inculturating marriage and Chisungu initiation rites would indeed be life-giving to Christian women in the context of contemporary challenges such as poverty, climate change, and STIs. It must be noted that there are different opinions on the desirability of inculturating female initiation rites into contemporary Zambian culture. Rasing is of the view that the process is necessary. He reasons that in the colonial past the rites were misjudged as contributing to immoral behaviour, whereas today, it is recognised that, instead, they may help to build sound moral standards.[12] It is assumed that initiation rites can help in the prevention of STIs by empowering women and promoting a positive morality in society. Women continue to stress the importance of female initiation ceremonies as they safeguard their important role as transmitters of culture.

The validity of inculturating initiation rites with the aim of empowering women is the subject of intensive discussion in countries like Malawi where attempts at inculturation have been made. Longwe is of the opinion that, while the Christian response to female initiation rites held among the Baptist Chewa women represents an effort to be open minded in respect of puberty rituals as rites of transition, the resulting ceremonies have many shortfalls.[13] They do not, for example, reflect the Chewa sense of identity and history.[14] Also, the church has omitted acknowledging the duties of initiation tutors as part of the church ministry. The result is that initiation tutors have lost respect and standing in church and community.[15] Moyo's research indicates that the inculturation of female initiation rites, when properly done, provides women with a safe space in which to exercise their leadership roles of initiating young women into adulthood. The initiates are empowered by receiving sex education, by celebrating womanhood, and by connecting with nature.[16] Evidently, there are values in marriage and Chisungu initiation rites that, if reclaimed and inculturated, can strengthen women in the face of contemporary challenges. What then is the position of the church in Zambia in this respect? As there are many Protestant churches in Zambia, I will limit myself to taking a cursory look at the UCZ.

9.3 THE POSITION OF THE UCZ ON INCULTURATION OF MARRIAGE AND FEMALE INITIATION RITES

The UCZ was formed on 16th January 1965. It incorporates the Church of Central Africa in Rhodesia (itself a union of the Church of Scotland and the London Missionary Society churches with the Union Church of the Copperbelt), the congregations of the Copperbelt Free Church Council, the Church of Barotseland, and the Zambia district of the Methodist Church.[17] After the union, the UCZ continued to adhere to the doctrines and the practices of the missionaries and adopted the constitution of the Presbyterian Church of Scotland making only a few changes. The new church maintained the stance of the missionaries on marriage, initiation rites, and sexuality.[18]

The missionaries of the London Missionary Society (LMS) who worked among the Bemba had banned marriage and Chisungu initiation rites along with other cultural practices. The Presbyterians at Lubwa mission and the Catholic mission in the north of Northern Rhodesia would punish women for performing initiation rites by suspending them.[19] The missionaries tended to prioritize the education of young men of whose technical skills they could put to use. Although the LMS proclaimed the sanctity of marriage, the cultural leadership roles of women were not upheld and the celebration of sex in marriage was undermined. All Christians were expected to abandon African culture.[20] The LMS and the Scottish missionaries opened training centres for women and girls at Mbeleshi and Lubwa, respectively. However, the courses focused exclusively on domestic science subjects and thus fostered the housebound position of women.[21]

The failure of the LMS and Scottish Presbyterian missionaries to inculturate those values of African culture that could empower women led to the Lumpa uprising of Alice Mulenga Lenshina. As Bujo observes, initiation rites are important because they constitute an educational institution in society.[22] The destruction of ancestral worship and the territorial shrines of which women were guardians, disempowered them further. During the Lumpa uprising, protesting women challenged the mission church to inculturate traditional ceremonies such as the Chisungu initiation rites so as to fulfill the needs of the Christian community. However, efforts in that direction died away soon after the uprising.[23] After its formation, the UCZ worked hard to reconcile former members of the Lumpa church with the mission churches, but the inculturation of Chisungu initiation was hardly attended to.[24]

While the UCZ maintained the missionary stance on female initiation rites, women themselves took the matter in hand and came to an outside-the-church arrangement. Today, they continue to hold initiation rituals for girls on reaching puberty and for those who are getting married. If held prior to the wedding, they combine the rites with a 'kitchen party.'[25] The insistence of women on the inculturation of marriage and Chisungu initiation rites in the context of prevalent STIs among Zambian women, indicates that the rites are perceived as empowering.

9.4 INCULTURATION OF MARRIAGE AND CHISUNGU INITIATION FOR THE EMPOWERMENT OF WOMEN

The call by women for the inculturation of initiation rites suggests an attempt to reclaim the status enjoyed by women in indigenous African Bemba culture. The demand indicates that there is a gap between the views of the church and the cultural perceptions of its members, especially women.[26] To bridge this gap, the church, particularly the UCZ, needs to revisit its position on the inculturation of marriage and female initiation rites.

Phiri's research underlines the importance of inculturated female initiation rites because they provide sex education to girls and women.[27] In addition to discussing aspects of motherhood, inculturated female initiation rites give women an opportunity to celebrate their womanhood. She adds: "Although the biblical teachings are meant to turn girls into submissive wives, certain good moral teachings can be sifted out and what empowers women should be passed on from one generation to the next."[28]

Based on the presence of positive values in marriage and Chisungu initiation as well, the rites could be turned into an effective tool for the empowerment of women, helping them to reclaim their identities as head of their families. However, if the UCZ attempts to inculturate Chisungu initiation rites, the church has to focus on those values of initiation that promoting equality of men and women. Doing so may open a window of opportunity for both genders, empowering them to meet current challenges head on. The various UCZ departments run projects coordinating community initiatives. Among these are HIV and AIDS programs.[29]

In the different congregations and presbyteries, there are committees and church groups such as mothers' guilds, men's Christian fellowships, and youths' Christian fellowships that contribute to social empowerment programs.[30] Some of the factors that fuel the spread of STIs are taboos on openly discussing sex, slow behavioural change, and gender inequality. In its response to issues contributing to the spread of HIV, the churches in Zambia, including UCZ, employ the 'ABC' rule (Abstain, Be faithful, Condomise).[31] Churches generally tend to emphasize against the risk of being infected during sexual intercourse. This approach has frequently served merely to heighten the shame and stigma associated with STIs and promoted judgmental attitudes towards affected individuals, especially women. The church preaches abstinence to the unmarried and faithfulness to the married.[32]

Unfortunately, promoting abstinence and faithfulness in a community where male headship is upheld makes women more vulnerable to infection with STIs because they are powerless to negotiate for safe sex. The church, therefore, needs to empower women, helping them to resist religio-cultural and social structures that promote gender inequality.[33] Van Klinken writes that the notion of male headship is strongly promoted by churches in Zambia. The concept of male headship has largely contributed to the kind of male behaviour that exposes their partners to STIs.[34] As Schmid points out, 'ABC' is meaningless for women in Africa. The wishes of their male partners prevail and women usually don't have the option to abstain or to suggest the use of condoms.[35] It is clear that, to achieve success in the prevention of STIs, the church has to address the issue of patriarchy and support a theology that enables women to celebrate their bodies as sacred. Also, the teaching of certain traditional values to men and women together should be considered by the church as a way of inculturating marriage and Chisungu initiation rites. Premarital socialisation and counselling, targeting men and women who intend to get married, may lead to increased egalitarianism in the community.

While women contribute in preparing young women for marriage, the church has not given them enough space to reclaim and introduce traditional values that may be of use to women in the contemporary world. In the UCZ, women are usually involved as matrons. The actual counselling is done by the minister and the marriage guidance committee.[36] This arrangement denies women the fulfilment of their traditional roles as tutors of the initiation and as social and religious leaders. Siwila observes that while the church tries its best to respond to social issues, it needs to address the real causes for the vulnerability of women.[37]

In this context, the church may consider the inculturation of the positive values of marriage and Chisungu initiation. Such an inculturation would provide the women's guilds with an adequate platform for sexual education and empowerment of both men and women. As Moyo argues, inculturating and reclaiming the authority and leadership of women in female initiation rites is necessary, because it is Christianity that has deprived women from the roles they used to perform in pre-colonial matrilineal societies. Inculturating the positive values of Chisungu will enable women to critique patriarchy in African culture from within and to resist patriarchal Christian and western ideologies that perpetuate the subordination of women in both church and society.[38]

In addition, inculturating marriage and Chisungu initiation rites may lead to the restoration of religious and social leadership positions of women as guards of territorial shrines. As mentioned above, indigenous marriage and Chisungu initiation rites are used to bring women in close contact with nature. Research indicates that the oppression and marginalisation of women and nature in Africa as a result of patriarchal Christian ideologies are intertwined.[39] Inculturating the rites may enable the church to come up with a theology that empowers women and that also fosters ecological justice. It could restore the connectedness of women with nature and allow them full, confident self-expression in initiation songs and dances and through sacred emblems.[40]

However, the inculturation of female initiation rites poses its own challenges. Fiedler mentions that African women experience certain parts of female initiation rites as problematic when a male priest participates in the ceremony, for example, the elongation of the labia.[41] Moyo laments that the inculturated female initiation rites among the Man'anja and the Yao people in Malawi have failed to provide lessons on sex that are sufficiently informative and explicit to help in the prevention of STIs.[42] This stipulates the need for the church in Zambia to preserve in its inculturated version of marriage and Chisungu initiation rites the traditional extensive instruction on sexual matters. In view of the prevalence of STIs, a theology of sexuality is needed that deconstructs the persistent myths around sexuality and the female body.[43] This will also increase women's understanding of Christian and medical perspectives on menstruation, thus freeing them of misconceptions. The church, when inculturating marriage and Chisungu initiation rites, needs to uphold the traditional role and status of the tutors of initiation (*bana chimbusa*). In other words, the organisation and execution of the rites should be entirely in the hands of women. Many members of the church send their children to indigenous marriage tutors because the church doesn't allow *bana chimbusa* to provide premarital counselling.[44] According to Fiedler, disregarding the cultural qualifications of the initiation tutors has led to the failure of inculturated female initiation rites to empower women. As a result, the tutors have lost respect in the church and the community.[45] Hinfelaar observes that 'kitchen parties' and inculturated forms of Chisungu initiation rites should not limit the use of marriage emblems to only those that teach about domestic and wifely duties of women. The emphasis must fall on the status and rights of women.[46]

In many churches, including the Catholic Church, women complain about male ministers organising lessons for women who are about to enter marriage. These complaints should be seen as protests by women who wish for the traditional position and autonomy of tutors of marriage and female initiation rites to be reclaimed. In response, the church should revive the indigenous model of teaching.

9.5 AN INDIGENOUS AFRICAN-CHRISTIAN MODEL OF MARRIAGE RULE

The Roman Catholic Church and some congregations in the UCZ have started drawing on African culture in their lessons to married couples. They have Christianised some lessons that used to be taught in traditional marriages. These lessons provide an example of an indigenous model of marriage that addresses both husband and wife. [47]

9.5.1 Rules applicable to the man
- A man should love his wife as Christ loves the church.
- A man should care for his wife.
- A man should not hide his financial income from his wife.
- A man should not fight or beat his wife.
- A man should be concerned with the health of his wife.
- A man should learn to communicate and find common ground with his wife.
- When a man differs with his wife, he should not insult his in-laws.

9.5.2 Rules applicable to the woman
- Find time to be with her husband after work.
- Discuss with her husband matters of fashion.
- In case of a conflict, the wife should not pack up and go to stay with her relatives or tell her husband to leave. Instead, she should look for solutions and reconciliation.
- Giving her husband love charms is bad.
- The wife should inform her husband when she wants to visit relatives or attend funerals.
- She should not get anything on credit without discussing it with her spouse.
- She must be economical with food and financial resources.
- If her husband poses problems, inform his relatives.

9.5.3 Rules applicable to both
- Invest gradually.
- Do not have extra-marital affairs.
- Seek the advice of doctors about family planning.

- Don't insult each other.
- Maintain cleanliness of body and home.
- Attend funerals.
- Do not envy other people.
- Maintain good relations with people.
- Spend time with your spouse and family.
- Buy gifts showing love for each other and have love meals (*ututemba cupo*).
- Be patient when disclosing sensitive information, such as concerning a funeral.
- Do not be a false witness.
- Care for your spouse when he/she is sick and inform his/her relatives if the sickness lasts.
- Do not keep secrets unnecessarily.
- Do not check the phone, computer, or Facebook account of your spouse unnecessarily. You may misunderstand information.
- Protect your spouse from your relatives.
- Show concern and care to relatives (*umutembo ufinina konse konse*).
- Have good friends.
- If you meet old friends of the opposite sex, quickly introduce them to your spouse to avoid suspicion.
- Show your children that you love each other.
- Be humble to people, especially elders.
- Shave each other's private parts.
- Use resources, especially money, wisely. Buy household goods and so on according to your financial capacity.
- Relatives should not be making decisions on your behalf.
- Be hospitable.
- Support each other in religious matters.

- Do not gossip with your relatives.
- Satisfy each other sexually and support each other when there is a problem of sexual malfunction.

9.6 CONCLUSION

Chapter nine assesses the importance of inculturating certain values of indigenous marriage an Chisungu initiation rites in the church. The chapter argues that by adhering to the teaching of European missionaries the Protestant churches in Zambia have not done well on the inculturation of marriage and Chisungu initiation rites. Given that women in pre-Christian Bemba society held leadership positions, the church's failure to inculturate marriage and Chisungu initiation has led to a disempowerment of women. Hence, by inculturating those values of indigenous marriage and Chisungu female initiation that promote equality with men and leadership roles of women can make women strong in the face of contemporary challenges such as poverty, climate change, and STIs. Besides, the inculturation of marriage and Chisungu initiation may enable the church to come up with a theology that deconstructs patriarchy and myths about marriage, sexuality, and menstruation while advancing mutuality in relationships.[48]

CHAPTER TEN

GENDER, MASCULINITY, AND PATRIARCHY: CONTINUITIES AND DISCONTINUITIES

10.1 INTRODUCTION

Tribes in Zambia have been culturally influenced by external forces such as colonization, Christianity, trade, migration, science, and technology. Western cultural, political, and religious views have changed the country. Much of what used to be the fabric of African communities has been lost because of Christianity. Africans were expected to abandon their cultural values.[1] As a result, age-old cultural practices disappeared or took on a new form conforming to the western-Christian worldview. This is how weddings and female initiation rites in Zambia got their contemporary shape, emerging from the interaction between western Christianity and indigenous cultures. To a large extent, these new forms have reinforced patriarchy, whereas, Bemba marriage and initiation rites in pre-colonial times were characterized by both positive and negative values as shown in the previous chapters.

10.2 GENDER

The values embedded in marriage and female initiation ceremonies play an important role in the transmission of knowledge, customs, and traditions. This includes music, dance, and dramatizations that usually are part of the ceremonies.[22]

A closer look at the wedding ceremonies practiced in Zambia in the past and today shows that there are both continuities and changes in forms and practices. Because of political, socio-economic, and socio-cultural changes, traditions have become mixed. It is difficult to find a purely traditional wedding ceremony in the urban areas of Zambia. Besides, today there are women who conduct rites for commercial purposes rather than to inculcate traditional values in initiates. In today's marriage ceremonies, women have to a large extent preserved traditional dances such as *imfunkutu,* but there is an abridgement of the repertoire.[3] In the Copperbelt or Lusaka provinces of Zambia, women may, for example, pick a Ngoni or Tonga song but use it for dancing *imfunkuti* which is no less than a betrayal of African culture.

The values taught to women in traditional wedding and female initiation rites have been blamed for contributing to male dominance in society. The current gender discourse in Zambia maintains that African culture contributes to gender based violence because of its emphasis on the subordinate position of women. It has also been established that the subordinate position of women in Zambia is the cause of the high HIV prevalence among women.[4] Zambia is one of the sub-Saharan countries hardest hit by the pandemic.[5] It is estimated that 14.3 percent of the adult population has been infected with the virus, the majority of whom (56 %) are women.[6] Hence, more women than men are living with HIV, and young women between fifteen and twenty-four years are as much as eight times more likely than men to be HIV positive.[7] Furthermore, about 60 percent of people newly infected through heterosexual transmission are infected within marriage and cohabitation.[8]

The pandemic, geographically and regarding the division between men and women, is not spread evenly. There is a higher infection rate in urban areas (23%) as compared to rural areas (11%).[9] This unevenness is also evident in the different provinces ranging from 6 percent in Northern Province to as high as 18 percent in Lusaka province.[10] Hence, the spread of the epidemic in Zambia suggests that there are many localized and divergent patterns that need to be understood and tackled with a variety of targeted interventions.[11]

At the root of the vulnerability of women to HIV infection is the problem of patriarchy that has led to gender inequality and socio-cultural practices that subordinate women to men.[12] The current discourse on marriage and sex in Zambia perpetuates the women's lower status in marriage and love relationships, and consequently, their greater exposure to STIs.[13] However, the current Zambian discourse on marriage and sex does not seem consistent with the values of African culture as taught in pre-colonial and pre-Christian Bemba society. Phiri and Nadar observe that it is not correct to look upon all African cultural practices as patriarchal. Some aspects of African culture contain potential criticism of patriarchy.[14] Why then is there in the current gender discourse in Zambia such a strong emphasis on the subordinate position of women?

10. 2. 1 Construction of gender in early childhood

In pre-colonial Zambian society, construction of gender identities started before the age of ten.[15] R. M. Kambole notes that girls of five and boys of ten years would begin to interact and play games together. They would, for example, play-act mock marriage (ukubuta ku mansansa). Thereby, the girls did imitate what they had seen their mothers do and the boys behaved like their fathers. Thus, boys and girls at play were equal to each other. However, as they grew up they began to pick up hints of how men and women were expected to behave. And soon, thereafter, girls stopped playing with boys. Instead, they began to perform the duties of grown-up women and men. Girls would start cooking for boys and the first signs of their subordination appeared.

In contemporary society, the construction of gender identities starts at the same age. Children pick up what they see their parents do. They also follow the behaviour of their peers at school. This is why parents and school should promote socialization and gender equality. Primary socialization takes place during infancy within the family. Through interaction with its family members, a child learns the mother tongue and a host of other basic behavioral patterns of the particular society that he belongs to. Each society has ways of training its younger members to adhere to its social values. Without this process, a child cannot develop such human behavior as is considered to be normal by a given society.

10. 2. 2 Construction of femininity at female common places

Traditionally, from the age of six to ten onwards, gender construction took place at Bemba common places called insaka for men and ichibwanse for women. At 'ichibwanse' women defined and reinforced what was perceived as the ideal woman (umwanakashi wabunyinu). This resulted in what may be referred to as hegemonic femininity. At female common meeting places, women reminded each other of the lessons they were taught during marriage and Chisungu initiation rites.

A woman who didn't attend such a common place was viewed as abnormal and uncultured (chitongo/chipelelo).

A common place for women

Simon Kapwepwe lists the subjects taught at women's meeting places as follows:

- Cooking
- Winnowing
- How to dress well
- Drawing water and collecting firewood
- Making fire
- Brewing beer
- Selecting and keeping seeds for planting
- Keeping one's house clean
- Keeping one's body clean
- What to do when menstruating
- Respect and humility
- Confidentiality
- Hospitality
- Proverbs and praises

- Revision of what was taught during puberty female initiation and marriage rituals
- Farming and home industries
- Motherhood
- Trade
- Leadership
- The need for a woman to be assertive (kashanga mu nshitolwa)
- Discipline, obedience, and respect to elders

The lessons assisted women to adequately fulfill their housekeeping and parenting duties. But they also taught them to be leaders in society. Some of the most important and influential decisions in communities were made at women's common meeting places.

Young women were familiarized with the use of specific herbs for healing purposes and for lengthening the labia. Some African societies practice female genital mutilation (FGM) of which there are three types. The first type consists of the removal of the clitoris. The second type involves the excision of the clitoris and the inner vaginal lips. The third type concerns removing the clitoris, the inner lips, the outer lips, and then sewing everything together leaving a very small opening for urination and menses. Women who undergo the third type of FGM, experience serious problems with menstruation and suffer terrible pain when having sexual intercourse or delivering a child.[16] However, the Bemba people of Zambia have never practised FGM.

Young girls were shown herbs that, when applied to the genitals, facilitate stretching the labia and promote vagina tightening and dryness. Girls were taken into the bush where women taught them about sex enhancing herbs. Some herbs could be chewed or taken as a drink to expedite the reaching of puberty. Medicines were applied to the face or smoked to attract the love of men. Charms or medicines could also be rubbed into a cut made into one's skin (ukulembelela).[17]

The issue of patriarchy or male headship as it occurs in western feminist discourse never arose. Women had no problem with men heading families, as long as they satisfied their wives sexually and provided for the needs of the family. If a man failed to do so, the wife automatically assume the role of head of the family. There was mutuality. An ideal woman was expected to be industrious and to overwhelm or inspire or dominate a man when having sex through her dancing techniques (ukuneng'a).

10. 2. 3 Construction of masculinity at male common meeting places

Bemba men had their own meeting places called insaka where they defined what made a real man. Thus, hegemonic masculinity was constructed and reinforced. Never to attend such a place made a man look foolish and abnormal (ifutu) in the eyes of the community. Simon Kapwepwe and R.M. Kambole describe the lessons taught to men as:

- Learning different arts and crafts as apprentices. Boys learned from the elders how to make baskets, reed marts, fish traps, and traps for animals and birds, axes, holes, how to build and roof houses, and make bullets for the gun called matzo roader (mututila).
- Communal life. If one person had some job to clear, the entire community assisted (ukulima iciima). Work, food, good moments, and sad moments were shared.
- Children were taught Bemba customs such as the need to respect elders and parents, how to live with neighbours, how to live with in-laws, how to relate to young men of your own

age, and how to relate to women.

- The need for a man to be brave.
- Kingship, how to be a good leader, to respect a leader and to know what type of food and gifts one offers to the king.
- Herbs to cure different ailments.
- Collecting firewood
- Herbs and medicine to make the penis strong, increase sperm count, cure impotence, or increase one's fertility.
- The origins of the Bemba people and their culture
- Hunting and fishing
- Proverbs and praises
- How to be a warrior during war.
- To be disciplined, obedient, and respectful towards elders.

Instruction took place in the bush where young men introduced them to sex-enhancing herbs, leaves, and roots of specific trees such as umusafwa, kafupa, indale, chimpampa, akasansu bwanga or umwenge. Certain medicines had to be soaked in a container and made into a drink. Young boys were shown medicines that could be applied to the face or smoked and that would attract women. An ideal man was expected to have sexual prowess. He was symbolically compared to the lion (mundu) and his role in life was to conquer a woman sexually.

10. 2. 4 Masturbation and homosexuality

Whether homosexuality and masturbation existed in Africa before the dawn of colonialism is debated. Masturbation is sexual self-stimulation by a man or woman. Homosexuality refers to having or manifesting sexual feelings for a member of one's own sex. Masturbation was common practice in Bemba society before colonialism. There were men and women who practised masturbation whenever it was impossible to have sex with someone else or when they felt a strong sex-drive.[19]

Masturbation was also used to determine the sexual prowess of young boys before or around puberty. Young boys would hold masturbation competitions in the bush under the tutorage of young men. A boy who ejaculated fast or whose sperm went further than that of others was considered a real man in the making (umwaume). Two or three boys might be made to stand alongside a ridge (uluputa) in the field. The boy whose sperm went over the ridge would be declared a winner. Women also masturbated in the fields using bananas. Older women might take a small boy and put his penis in their vagina while she masturbated. There was no question of real penetration but it helped the women to reach orgasm.

In pre-colonial times, homosexuality was also a common practice among the Bemba. Almost nothing has been written about it because matters of sex were not discussed in public. In addition, Bemba culture emphasised heterosexuality for the sake of procreation and continuity of family lineages. Bemba beliefs concerning sexuality are linked to their beliefs about the cycle of birth, physical growth, maturity, old age, and death. It is believed that sperm is placed within a woman by ancestors to safeguard the lineage, hence, the emphasis on heterosexual marriage. At the same time sexual pleasure played an important role in Bemba culture, and both men and women were taught to maximise sexual pleasure in marriage.

Homosexual acts, although not openly discussed, were acceptable in certain circumstances.[20] A woman could masturbate or involve in a homosexual act with another woman using a banana. This was accepted if her husband was away for a long time and she did not want to have sex with his cousins or brothers. Young women before marriage could do the same. Men could also have anal sex usually with someone younger or with a small boy.[21] If a man was not satisfied with masturbation and there was no woman available, he could find a young boy and ejaculate in between his legs or have anal sex.[22] For some kings, sex with men was part of their cultural practice.

By and large, what in western parlance is called homosexuality, masturbation, and sodomy were practised in pre-colonial Bemba society and deemed acceptable for reasons of pleasure and to discourage adultery. There was, however, a taboo on discussing such matters in public. Elderly people were aware that these things happened. The shame and stigma attached to these practices is due to the western and Christian understanding of them. The colonial government introduced laws that defined homosexuality as deviant behaviour for which one could be imprisoned.[23] Christianity condemned both homosexuality and masturbation as sins.

10.3 PATRIARCHY IN ZAMBIAN MARRIAGE RITES

Zambian society has changed since pre-colonial times. Sociologists note that a society may undergo emergent change, transformative change, and projectable change. Emergent change refers to what people learn from experiencing day-to-day life, consciously or subconsciously, as individuals, families, and communities. Transformative change is the consequence of a crisis which makes people adjust their beliefs and practices while projectable change implies the conscious effecting of change.[24] When changes occur a society may keep some practices and abandon or adjust others.[25]

Christianity and social movements such as migration and changing one's geographical location have resulted in the mixing of cultures in Zambia. The tendency to leave rural areas and settle in cities, coupled with the introduction of western education, has affected people's way of life and worldviews. Secularization and scientific developments similarly have affected the way people think and has affected their attitudes to legitimacy and authority, thus influencing social structures, systems, and values.[26] Technology has brought to light information that used to be safeguarded as traditional secrets. In short, many social, political, and religious factors have changed Zambian culture, including the form and practice of marriage and female initiation rites.

In urban areas, for example, Zambian women have invented the 'kitchen party.' The food-giving ceremony (amatebeto) has been changed. Amatebeto refers to a function organised for the groom. As in pre-colonial times the groom is still expected to get his food at his in-law's place, but the practice has nowadays become more of a commercial venture for the modern tutors (banachimbusa or alangizi in Nyanja). The kitchen party is for the bride and is held before the wedding or on the same day after the marriage blessing in church.[27] The party includes lessons on sexual matters, the submission of the wife, general cleanliness, and industriousness.[28] Because of the commercialisation of kitchen parties and an understanding of Christian marriage and sexual values, the teaching, today, is well removed from what traditional Bemba culture taught. The loss of these ancient values is responsible for patriarchy, defilement, and GBV in marriage. A comparison of the songs sung during modern kitchen parties and those performed during indigenous marriage and Chisungu initiation confirms this.

Mwana alelila ibeele	The child is crying for the breast
Wishi alelila akanena	The father is crying for the vagina
Namukobwa	I am in trouble
Nakobwa pabili	I am entangled

| Namukobwa | I am in trouble |
| Nakobwa pabili | I am entangled |

The words imply that the mother should not neglect her baby for the sake of the father. A man may start demanding sex and attention from his wife forgetting that she is breastfeeding the child. The song indicates that it was the woman who had to judge whether the time was right for sex. Sex was not allowed when the woman was menstruating, sick, or in the early months of breast feeding. Women could use beads of different colors to communicate their availability to their husbands. Kitchen party songs, however, send a different message.

Muntombe bwino	Fuck me good
Muntombe bwino	Fuck me good
Ine ndi mulwele	I am sick
Soswe lishili	Clitoris is mad
Tamona bukala nelyo alwele	It rejoices to see the penis even when it's sick

According to this text, women should always be ready for sex, even when they are sick. If they don't, the husbands will find other women. When it comes to sex, this song emphasizes, there is no 'I am sick' or 'I am menstruating.' In other words, the song presents women as sex objects and it justifies patriarchy and extra-marital affairs. GBV in Zambia has occurred because of the notion that a woman cannot say 'no' to sex with her husband or negotiate for safe sex practices. Another traditional song used to give women certain powers.

| Intanda | Stars |
| Ulaasha intanda ubushiku | You light the stars at night |

| Ulantuka ukashika | You revile me obscenely, you red |

This initiation song warns the groom not to have sex with his wife when she is menstruating. He should not insult his wife by mentioning the menstrual blood but show her understanding.

Some songs performed during kitchen parties are overly concerned with sex and seem to turn women into sex machines for the benefit of men.

Amatako yandi ine	My buttocks
Yachinsense yachinsense amatako yandi	My buttocks are small
Akantu ni apa	But my strength is here [vagina]
Epo nakilisha ee	That's where I please...
Epo nakilisha kubalume bandi	That's where I please my husband

In other words, the buttocks do not matter and have no purpose; but the vagina does because that is where the husband finds pleasure. The song presents women as having been created for no other purpose but to please men. Making sex into a central concern has caused Zambian men to use all sorts of sex-enhancing herbs such as Congo dust and mutototo to satisfy and conquer women sexually. As opposed to this contemporary trend, the lessons taught by songs in traditional Bemba society did accentuate the well-being of women. Tutors would strike a balance between the duties of husband and wife; thus, the song:

Chiboni musuma	The Euphorbia tree
Iwe mune, waleta chitonfwa	You have brought a stubborn child
Naine, nafyala chintomfwa	I have born a stubborn child also
Fyakumana na chitomfwa	They match

In other words, there should be mutuality in marriage. The husband should look upon his wife as beautiful and vice versa. Chiboni is a giant euphorbia tree, but it was also the name of the legendary beautiful wife of a Bemba king. The song implies that the husband should treasure his wife, and should they have differences, they were expected to reconcile and forgive each other, because no one on earth is perfect.

What comes to the fore is that, nowadays, the lessons given during kitchen parties in Zambia promote patriarchy and the objectification of women. This is in contradiction to efforts made by the Women's Lobby Group and the Zambian government to promote gender equality and curb GBV. NGOs and government need to develop a strategy through which some of the life-giving lessons offered in pre-colonial and matrilineal Bemba society can be reclaimed. Research indicates that domestic violence and abuse of women stem from the gender stratification in society. In matrilineal, matrifocal, and bilateral societies gender stratification is less prominent and women may fulfil important roles in the economy and social life.[29] In present-day Zambian society, there is much to be said for a multi-sectorial and multi-dimensional approach to the fight against patriarchy because domestic violence, for example, is just one of a whole series of interconnected manifestations of patriarchy.[30]

10.4 CONCLUSION

Chapter ten discusses how form, structure, and purpose of marriage and female initiation rites in Zambia have changed since pre-colonial times. There are continuities and discontinuities. The chapter confirms what has been established in previous chapters, namely, that in pre-colonial Bemba communities, the concept of femininity was not in any way associated with passivity or subordination on the part of the wife. Rather, being a real woman implied a form of agency to satisfy the needs of husband and family. Similarly, masculinity as a concept did not hint at any form of abuse of women whatsoever. It expressed the ability to satisfy the needs of wife and family. A real man had to live up to the challenge of being a responsible husband, lover, protector, and care-taker of the family.

CHAPTER ELEVEN

GENERAL CONCLUSION

11.1 INTRODUCTION

Chapter eleven summarises the study and presents a synthesis of findings. By analysing the aims, forms, practices, and gendered values of marriage and Chisungu initiation rites, I expected to obtain answers to the question of whether reclaiming and inculturating values of those rituals as they used to be celebrated in pre-colonial times could empower women in Zambia today in the face of many challenges. My question was worded as follows: *What gendered cultural values can be reclaimed from indigenous marriage and female Chisungu initiation rites to critique patriarchy and empower women in the context of contemporary challenges such as poverty, climate change, cervical cancer, and HIV and AIDS?*

The question was premised on the hypothesis that such values exist. A number of conclusions have been drawn from the research findings. These conclusions lead to new questions that will necessitate further research.

11.2 CONCLUDING REMARKS

This study presents a discussion of the marriage and Chisungu initiation rites among the Bemba people of Zambia, in pre- and post-colonial times and from a gendered perspective. The aim is to establish how gendered values of these ancient rituals can be reclaimed and integrated into contemporary Zambian culture. The study concludes that a revival of the positive values of indigenous marriage and Chisungu initiation rites will make it possible to critique patriarchy from within society and may empower women in the context of contemporary challenges.

In chapter one the research problem is introduced and located within the body of current research by anthropologists, sociologists, and African (women) theologians. The chapter offers the theoretical framework and the methodology used.

Chapter two lists concepts and theories that are used in research on culture and gender conducted in the disciplines of sociology, anthropology, and religious studies. This provided the tools for determining how social change has affected form and practice of marriage and female initiation rites in Zambia.

Chapter three offers a survey of feminism, its origins, its development, and the different ideological positions of feminists. The chapter accentuates the need to define gender, patriarchy, and feminism using African thought forms.

Chapter four defines ritual, explaining how it is related to beliefs, ideologies, and concepts of power. It is pointed out that marriage and female initiation rites have power to allow new members, that is, the newly adults, into the community and to define what their roles and behaviour in that community should be.

Chapter five is concerned with the function, form, and practices of Chisungu female initiation rites. The cultural setting of the Bemba people as a matrilineal society is described. Bemba people conduct initiation ceremonies at puberty or/and at marriage. A comparison of past and present reveals continuities as well as changes in structure and content of Chisungu initiation. In chapter five, it is argued that, given the inclusion in Chisungu initiation of lessons on social and religious leadership roles of women, its influence goes beyond the mere provision of sex education. This leads me to conclude that if lessons promoting gender equality and access of women to leadership roles were part of a contemporary initiation program, it could open a window of opportunity for the empowerment of women, enabling them to deal with the serious challenges facing them.

Chapter six presents Bemba marriage initiation rites. It is argued that despite having been banned by missionaries, indigenous marriage and Chisungu initiation rites continue to be celebrated and remain an important, culturally accepted source of information on sexual morality and on issues concerning the roles and status of women and men.

Chapter seven highlights the gendered cultural values of marriage and Chisungu initiation rites, focusing on the education provided by initiation tutors and on the traditional gendered roles of Bemba women. The chapter demonstrates the symbolic meanings implied in the rites and the interpretation of sacred emblems and initiation songs. Chapter seven makes clear that while various aspects of initiation accentuate the submission of women to men, indigenous marriage and Chisungu initiation rites simultaneously offer values that promote gender equality and leadership roles of women. Such values, if reclaimed, can empower women today, for example, in the context of the prevention of STIs. In this chapter, I argue that certain positive values of traditional Chisungu initiation rites have lost their potential because of external factors such as the introduction of Christianity, elements of western civilisation, and interaction of Bemba culture with other patriarchal African cultures, resulting in the current overwhelming emphasis on the submission of women to men.

In chapter eight, the potential advantages of retrieving the gendered values of marriage and Chisungu initiation for the purpose of women's empowerment are discussed. I argue that practices such as vagina tightening, inspection for labia elongation, taboos relating to sex and menstrual blood as well as misconceptions about married relationships need to be revised or discarded since they promote the subordinate position of women in marriage and society. On the other hand, there are practices that can be successfully retrieved to critique patriarchy from within the society, thus, empowering women in the context of, for example, the prevention of STIs. These values will positively effect the economic status of women and their right to protest and 'talk back' so that they can negotiate for safe sex. In addition, the adoption of such values may make an end to virginity inspection and delay the sexual debut. The chapter also states that in view of health hazards such as HIV and its impact on women, initiation tutors need to be equipped with a good deal of knowledge on STIs so that the sex education they provide will be solidly based.

Chapter nine assesses the possibilities of inculturating marriage and Chisungu initiation rites to improve women's ability to deal with contemporary challenges. The chapter highlights that by adhering to the teachings and doctrines of the European missionaries, the UCZ has neglected the potential of Chisungu initiation rites. While in pre-Christian Bemba society women played leadership roles, the position taken by the church has left women in post-colonial society disempowered. My argument is that inculturating those values of indigenous Chisungu initiation rites that empower women may help them to enforce safe sex practices, thus, establishing some control over the rampant spread of STIs. It may also enable the church to promote a theology that deconstructs patriarchy and mythical beliefs about marriage, sexuality, and menstruation while advancing mutuality in relationships.

Chapter ten analyses changes in Zambian society that have led to the contemporary forms and practices of marriage and female initiation rites which strengthen patriarchy and the objectification of women. It is argued that the current domineering emphasis on the sexual submission of women to men is not always consistent with lessons given to initiates during marriage and female initiation rites in pre-colonial, pre-Christian Bemba society. Chapter eleven offers a conclusion based on the findings of this study and raises new questions for further research.

11.3 NEW QUESTIONS RAISED BY THE STUDY

The present study argues that marriage and Chisungu initiation rites offer gendered values that, if reclaimed, may empower women in the context of contemporary challenges such as the prevention of STIs. This suggests that there may exist other cultural practices in African culture that can open windows of opportunity to empower people. There is a lot to research, learn, and possibly, borrow from African culture.

Second, the study indicates the religious, social, and political meanings hidden in songs and marriage emblems that feature in indigenous marriage and Chisungu initiation rites. Further research into the aims and the significance of marriage in African culture is called for and may well enrich Christianity's understanding of, and respect for, African worldviews.

Third, one of this study's focal points is that women in pre-colonial, pre-Christian Bemba society held religious and social leadership positions. It is suggested that an inculturation of marriage and Chisungu initiation rites in the church would create awareness that women can, and should, carry responsibility in church and society, fulfilling roles equal to those of men. The adoption of certain values of indigenous initiation will put women in a stronger position concerning the ecological crisis and the marginalisation of the natural world of which the results impact especially on the daily lives of African women.

Last, the study raises the negotiation of gender roles. Marriage and Chisungu initiation rites teach brides and grooms together about female and male roles in marriage and in life using sacred emblems to clarify lessons. On the basis of this particular feature of initiation, namely, the sharing of instruction on married life, women and men are made aware of the possibility to discuss together their roles in their relationship and in the wider society. Connected to this is the issue of creating a sexual ethic that is empowering and life-giving to both men and women.

11.4 CONCLUSION

This study is an attempt to unveil gendered values in traditional marriage and female Chisungu initiation rites that, if retrieved and inculturated in contemporary Zambian Christianity, can stimulate criticism of patriarchy from within the community and promote egalitarianism. The study shows that the outlook of pre-colonial Bemba society was not completely or irredeemably dominated by patriarchy. While patriarchy was present, there were many values that supported leadership roles of women. That both men and women could fulfill positions of public responsibility is confirmed by Taylor. Taylor, however, cautions not to overstate the nature of pre-colonial gender relations as being harmonious and allowing for women's empowerment although this was to a certain degree true in specific areas and for certain tribes.[1] He states that among some Zambian tribes women were given an amount of power and that this situation was negatively influenced by the arrival of colonialism and Christianity which diminished the status of women or wives while elevating those of men or husbands.[2] Industrialisation also contributed to the suppression of the leadership roles of women. Considerable amounts of unskilled and semi-skilled black labour were needed in the mines in the Central and Copperbelt Provinces. Women were left behind in the villages where maintaining their homes and providing for their families were their primary responsibilities.[3] Because indigenous marriage and female Chisungu initiation rites continue to function as cultural resources, providing education on matters of sex and the social and religious roles of women in Zambia, it is preferable not to think of legislating against them, but rather to welcome their activities, allow for adaptation, and appreciate the opportunities they offer for the empowerment of Zambian women today.

BIBLIOGRAPHY

Abbey, R.T. 2001. Rediscovering Ataa Naa Nyonmo – The Father – Mother God. In Njoroge and Dube (eds.). *Talitha cum! Theologies of African women.* Pietermaritzburg: Cluster Publications, 140-159.

Ackerman D. 2006. From mere existence to tenacious endurance – Stigma, HIV/AIDS and a feminist theology of praxis. In Phiri Isabel and Nadar Sarojini (eds.). African women, religion, and health: Essays in honour of Mercy Amba Ewudziwa Oduyoye. Maryknoll, NY: Orbis, 221-242.

Allen, J. 2008. Mabel Shaw's theology in the context of her work as a Christian missionary teacher in Northern Rhodesia, 1915-1940. Feminist Theology 16(2): 194-210.

Anderson, B. 2007. The Politics of Homosexuality in Africa. *Africana* 1: 123-136.

Bah, I. 2005. *Gender inequality and HIV/AIDS in Zambia: A study of the links between gender inequality and women's vulnerability to HIV/AIDS.* Huddinge: ISNJ.

Boas, T.C. 2007. Conceptualising continuity and change: The composite-standard model of path dependence. *Journal of theoretical politics* 19(1): 33-54,33.

Bolink, P. 1967. *Towards church union in Zambia. A study of missionary co-operation and church union efforts in central Africa.* Franeker: T. Wever.

Bruce, P. 2003. "The mother's cow": A study of Old Testament references to virginity in the context of HIV/AIDS in South Africa. In Phiri, I., Haddad, B., and Masenya, M. (eds.). *African women, HIV, AIDS and faith communities.* Pietermaritzburg: Cluster Publications.

Bujo, B. 1992. *African theology in its social context.* New York: Orbis.

Chondoka, Y.A. 1988. Traditional marriage in Zambia. Ndola: Mission press.

Corbeil, J.J. 1982. *Mbusa. Sacred emblems of the Bemba.* London: Ethnographic Publishers.

Cameron, E., and Jordan, M. 2006. Playing with the future: children and rituals in North-Western province of Zambia. In Ottenberg, Simon, and Binkley, David (eds.). *African children masquerade. Playful performers.* London: Transaction Publishers, 237-246.

Childress, J.F. 1986. Anthropology and ethics. In Childress, J.F., and Macquarrie J. (eds.). *Dictionary of Christian ethics.* London: SCM Press, 34-35.

Denis, P. 2003. Sexuality and AIDS in Southern Africa. *Journal of theology for Southern Africa* 113(March): 63-77.

Dennis, P. 2000. *Orality, memory and past: Listening to the voices of black clergy under colonialism and apartheid.* Pietermaritzburg: Cluster Publications.

Douglas, M. 1966: *Purity and danger: An analysis of the concepts of pollution and taboo.* London: Routledge.

Epstein, A.L. 1981. *Urbanisation and kinship: The domestic domain on the copperbelt of Zambia 1950-1956.* London: Academic Press.

Fiedler, K. 1996. *Christianity and African culture. Conservative German protestant missionaries in Tanzania, 1900-1940.* Leiden: Brill.

Fiedler, N.R. 2005. *Coming of age: A Christianised initiation for women in Southern Malawi.* Zomba: Kachere.

Fiorenza, E.S. 1997. Discipleship of equals: Reality and visions. In Kanyoro Musimbi (eds). *In search of a round table. Gender, Theology and Church leadership.* Geneva: WCC ppublications.

Garvey, B. 1994. *Bembaland church: Religious and social change in South Central Africa, 1891-1964.* New York: E.J. Brill.

Gnanadason, A. 1993. *No longer a secret: The church and violence against women.* Geneva: WCC publications.

Gomes, E. 1996. Sexuality and the well-being of women. In Kanyoro, M., and Njoroge, N. (eds). *Groaning in faith. African women in the household of God.* Nairobi: Acton Publishers.

Guedes, J.S. 2006. Bali fye umubili umo: Amafundisho ya cupo. Ndola: Mission Press.

Haddad, B. 2003. Choosing to remain silent: Links between gender violence, HIV, AIDS and the South African church. In Phiri, I, Haddad, B., and Masenya, M. (eds). *African women, HIV/AIDS and faith communities.* Pietermaritzburg: Cluster Publications,149-167.

Haddad, B. 2006. "We pray but we cannot heal": Theological challenges posed by the HIV/AIDS crisis. *Journal of Theology for Southern Africa* 125(1): 80-90.

Haddad, B. 2008. Surviving the HIV and AIDS epidemic in South Africa: Women living and dying, theologising and being theologised. *Journal of Theology for Southern Africa* 131(1): 47-57.

Harrison, A. 2005. *Young people and HIV/AIDS in South Africa: prevalence of infection, risk factors and social context.* Cambridge: Cambridge New Press.

Hastings, A. 1976. *African Christianity: An essay in interpretation.* Southampton: The Camelot Press.

Heath, J. 2009. *The need for comprehensive multi-faceted interventions.* Geneva: EAA.

Health line. Female reproductive organs. http://www.healthline.com/human-body-maps/female-reproductive-organs. Accessed 12/12/15.

Hinfelaar, H. 1994. *Bemba-speaking women of Zambia in a century of religious change (1892-1992)*. New York: Brill. Ikechukwu, P.O. 2008. An African moral theology of inculturation: Methodological considerations. *Theological studies* 69(3): 583-608.

Kabonde, P.M. 1996. Widowhood in Zambia: The effects of ritual. In Kanyoro, M., and Njoroge, N. (eds.). *Groaning in faith. African women in the household of God*. Nairobi. Acton Publishers.

Kambole, R.M. 1974. *Nkobekela te cupo/Engagement is not formal marriage*. Lusaka: ZEPH.

Kambole, R M. 1980. *Ukufunda umwana kufikapo*/Teach the child without beating about the bush. Lusaka: ZEPH.

Kangwa, J. 2011. *Reclaiming the values of female initiation rites as a strategy for HIV prevention: A gendered analysis of Chisungu initiation rites among the Bemba people of Zambia*. MTh Thesis, University of KwaZulu-Natal.

Kanyoro, M. 1996. 'Feminist theology and African culture'. *Violence against women*. Nairobi: Acton Publishers.

Kanyoro, M. 2001. Engendered communal theology: African women's contribution to theology in the 21st century. In Njoroge and Dube (eds.). *Talitha cum! Theologies of African women*. Pietermaritzburg: Cluster Publications.

Kanyoro, M. 2002. *Introducing Feminist Cultural Hermeneutics: An African perspective*. Sheffield: Sheffield Academic Press.

Kapungwe, A. 2003. Traditional cultural practices of imparting sex education and the fight against HIV/AIDS: The case of initiation ceremonies for girls in Zambia. *African Sociological Review* 7(1): 35-52.

Kapwepwe, S.M. 1967. *Shalapo canicandala*/Goodbye old grass. Lusaka: ZEPH.

Kaunda, C. 2010. Reclaiming the feminine image of God in Lesa. Implications for Bemba Christian women at the Evangelical

Assembly of God church in the post-missionary era. *Journal of Constructive Theology* 16(1):5-29.

Kaunda, C. 2010b. *Creation as a dwelling place of God: A critical analysis of an African biocentric theology in the works of Gabriel M. Sotiloane.* Unpublished Master's Thesis. University of Kwa Zulu-Natal.

Kibera, L.W., and Kimoti, A. 2007. *Fundamentals of sociology of education with reference to Africa.* Nairobi: University of Nairobi Press.

Kottak, C.P. 2002. *Anthropology: The exploration of human diversity.* 9th edition. Boston: McGraw Hill.

Kurian, M. 2004. "The HIV and AIDS pandemic changing perceptions on sexuality in faith communities". *Ecumenical Review* 56(4): 432-436.

La Fontaine, J. 1982. *Introduction.* In Richards, Audrey. Chisungu: A girl's initiation ceremony among the Bemba of Zambia. London: Tavistock, page xvii-xxxvii.

La Fontaine, J. 1986. *Initiation.* Manchester: Manchester University Press.

Landman, C. 1998. African women's theologies. In Maimela and Konic (eds.). *Initiation into theology: The varieties of theology and hermeneutics.* Pretoria: J.L. Van Schalk Publishers, 137-140.

Lindsey, L.L. 2011. Gender roles: A sociological perspective. 5th edition. New York: Pearson, 4. http://www.pearsonhighered.com/assets/hip/us/hip_us_pearsonhighered/samplechapter/0132448300.pdf. Accessed 16/12/15.

Longwe, M. 2003. *From Chinamwali to Chilangizo: the Christianisation of pre-Christian Chewa initiation rites in the Baptist convention of Malawi.* Unpublished Masters Dissertation. University of Kwa Zulu-Natal.

Lumbwe, K. 2013. Indigenous mfunkutu and contemporary ubwinga (wedding) music of the Bemba-speaking people of Zambia: Continuity and change. *Journal of the musical arts in Africa* 10:71-101.

Maluleke, T. 2001. African "Ruths". Ruthless Africa: Reflections of an African Modecai. In Musa Dube (ed.). *Other ways of reading. African women and the bible.* Geneva: WCC publications.

Masaiti, N.B. 2007. *African indigenous churches and polygamy in the context of HIV and AIDS: The case of the Mutima church in Zambia.* Unpublished Master's Thesis.

Masenya, M. 2003. Trapped between two "canons": African-South African Christian women in the HIV/AIDS era. In Phiri, Isabel et al (eds). *African women, HIV/AIDS and faith communities.* Pietermaritzburg: Cluster Publications, 113-127.

Masenya, M. 2010. All from the same source? Deconstructing a (male) anthropocentric reading of Job (3) through an eco-bosadi lens. *Journal of Theology for Southern Africa* 137 (July): 46-60.

Martey, E. 1993. *African Theology. Inculturation and Liberation.* Maryknoll: Orbis.

Marx, K. 1884. *The communist manifesto.* London: Penguin Books.

Mbozi, P. 2000. *The impact of negative cultural practices on the spread of HIV/AIDS in Zambia.* Lusaka: UNZA.

MOH/NAC. 2010. *Zambia country report. Monitoring the Declaration of Commitment on HIV and AIDS and the universal access.* Submitted to the United Nations General Assembly special session on AIDS declaration of commitment on 31/03/10.

Moyo, F. 2005. Sex, gender, power and HIV/AIDS in Malawi: Threats and challenges to women being Church. In Phiri and Nadar (eds). *On being Church: African women's voices and visions.* Geneva: WCC publications, 127-145.

Moyo, F. 2009. *A Quest for women's sexual empowerment through education in an HIV and AIDS context.* Unpublished PhD Thesis. University of Kwa Zulu-Natal.

Moyo, L. 2007. *Widowhood rituals, African Lutherans and HIV prevention: A gendered study of the experiences of widows in the Kamwala Evangelical*

Lutheran church in Zambia. Unpublished Master's Thesis.

Mutambara, M. 2006. African women Theologies critique inculturation. In Antonio Edward (ed.). *Inculturation and post-colonial discourse in African theology*. New York: Peter Lang, 173-186.

Oduyoye, M. 1986. *Hearing and knowing: Theological reflections on Christianity in Africa*. New York: Orbis.

Oduyoye, M. 1999. A coming home to myself. The childless woman in the West African space. In Farley, Margaret, and Jones, Serene (eds.). *Liberating Eschatology. Essays in honour of Letty M. Russell*. Louisville: Westminster John Knox Press.

Oduyoye, M. 1995. *Daughters of Anowa. African women and patriarchy*. Maryknoll: Orbis.

Oduyoye, M. 2004. *Beads and strands. Reflections of an African woman on Christianity in Africa*. Maryknoll: Orbis books.

Orger, L.M. 1991. *"Where a scattered flock gathered". Ilondola*. Ndola. Mission press.

Onsei-Bonsu, J. 2005. *The inculturation of Christianity in Africa*. Frankfurt am Main: Lang.

Parpart, J.L. 1994. Where Is Your Mother?: Gender, Urban Marriage, and Colonial Discourse on the Zambian Copperbelt, 1924-1945. *The International Journal of African Historical Studies* 27(2):241-271.

Phiri, I. 1997. Doing theology in the community: The case of African women theologians in the 1990s. *Journal of theology for southern Africa* 99:68-76.

Phiri, I. 2000. *Women, Presbyterianism and Patriarchy. Religious experiences of Chewa women in central Malawi*. Blantyre: CLAIM.

Phiri, I. 2000b. 'Stand up and be counted: Identity, spirituality and theological education in my journey of faith'. In Denise Ackerman, Eliza Getman, Hantie cotze and Judy Tobler (eds). *Claiming our footprints: South African women reflect on context, identity and spirituality*. Stellenbosch: EFSA institute for theological and interdisciplinary research, 145-160.

Phiri, I. 2003. African women of faith speak out in an HIV/AIDS era. In Phiri, I., Haddad, B., and Masenya, M. (eds). *African women, HIV/ AIDS and faith communities. Pietermaritzburg: Cluster Publications, 3-20*

Phiri, I. 2006. Dealing with the trauma of sexual abuse. A gender-based analysis of the testimonies of female traditional healers in Kwa Zulu-Natal. *In Phiri, Isabel, and Nadar, Sarojini (eds). African women, religion and health. Essays in honour of Mercy Amba Ewudzima Oduyoye.* Pietermaritzburg. Cluster Publications, 113-130.

Phiri, I., and Nadar, S. 2010. Talking back to religion and HIV and AIDS using an African feminist missiological framework: Sketching the contours of the conversation. *Journal of constructive theology* 16(2):8-24.

Poewe, K. 1981. *Matrilineal ideology. Male and female dynamics in the Luapula, Zambia.* London: Academic Press Inc.

Rakoczy, S. 2004. *In her name: Women doing theology.* Pietermaritzburg: Cluster Publications.

Rasing, T.1995. *Passing on the rites of passage: Girls' initiation rites in the context of an urban Roman Catholic community on the Zambian Copperbelt.* Leiden: Avebury.

Rasing, T. 2006. *HIV/AIDS and sex education among the youth in Zambia: Towards behavioural change*. http://asc.leidenuniv.nl/pdf/ paper091022003.pdf. Accessed 13/04/11

Reeler, D. 2007. *A three-fold theory of social change and implications for practice, planning, monitoring and evaluation.* Cape Town: Centre for developmental practice, 1-33.

Reuther, R. 1983. *Sexism and God-talk: Towards a feminist theology.* London: SCM Press.

Reuther, R. 1993. Ecofeminism: Symbolic and social connections of the oppression of women and domination of nature. In Adams, C.J. (ed.). *Ecofeminism and the sacred.* New York: Continuum, 13-23.

Richards, I.A. 1982. *Chisungu: A girl's initiation ceremony among the Bemba of Zambia*. London: Tavistock.

Roberts, A. 1973. *A history of the Bemba. Political growth and change in north eastern Zambia before 1900*. London: Longman.

Rotberg, R. 1965. *Christian missionaries and the creation of Northern Rhodesia 1880-1924*. Princeton: Princeton University Press.

Russell, L. 1993. *Church in round: Feminist interpretation of the church*. Louisville: Westminster.

Siwila, L. 2005. *African women, hospitality and HIV/AIDS: The case of the Mothers' Union of St. Margaret's United church of Zambia*. Unpublished Master's Thesis. University of Kwa Zulu-Natal.

Siwila, L. 2011. Problematising a 'norm': A religio-cultural gender analysis of child marriage in the context of HIV and AIDS. *Journal of Gender and Religion in Africa* 17(1): 27-49.

Siwila, L. 2011b. *Culture, gender, and HIV and AIDS: United Church of Zambia's response to traditional marriage practices*. Unpublished PhD Thesis. University of Kwa Zulu-Natal.

Schmid, B. 2005. *Sexuality and religion in the time of AIDS*. Cape Town: ARSRC.

Taylor, S.D. 2006. *Culture and customs of Zambia*. London: Greenwood Press.

Thelen, K. 2003. How institutions evolve: Insights from comparative historical analysis. In Mahoney, J., and Ruschemeyer (eds.). *Comparative historical analysis in the social sciences*. New York: Cambridge University Press, 208-240.

Touwen, A. 1984. *'I'm suffering'. A pilot study of the position of female heads-of-households in a rural Copperbelt community in Zambia*. Groningen: University of Groningen.

Turner, V.W. 1981. Encounter with Freud. The making of a comparative symbologist. In Spindler, G.D. (ed.). *The meaning of a psychological anthropologist*. California: University of California Press, 558-583.

Turner, V.W. 1982. *Celebration, studies in festivals and ritual.* Washington: Smithsonian Institute Press.

Turner, V.W. 1967. *The forest of symbols: Aspects of Ndembu ritual.* Ithaca NY: Cornell University Press.

Turner, V.W. 1969. *The ritual process: Structure and anti-structure.* Chicago: Aldine.

UCZ Constitution. 2004. *The constitution, rules and regulations of the United Church of Zambia.* Lusaka: UNZA Press.

UCZ HIV/AIDS policy. 2006. Synod community development department of the United Church of Zambia. Lusaka, Zambia.

UCZ Synod. 2008. *Minutes of the 24th Synod meeting of the United Church of Zambia held at Diakonia centre, Kabwe from 1st to 6th June, 2008.*

UNAIDS 2009 update http://www.unaids.org/en/knowledgecentre/ HIVData/Epiupdate/EpiupdArc. Accessed 04/08/2011

Van Klinken, A. 2011. Transforming masculinities towards gender justice in an era of HIV and AIDS. Plotting the pathways. In Haddad, Beverley (ed.). *Religion and HIV and AIDS. Charting the terrain.* Pietermaritzburg: UKZN Press.

Van Klinken, A. 2011. Male headship as male agency: An alternative understanding of a 'patriarchal' African Pentecostal discourse on masculinity. *Religion and Gender* 1(1): 104-124.

Wamwue, G. 1996. Women and taboo among the Kikuyu people. In Kanyoro, M., and Njoroge, N. (eds). *Groaning in faith. African women in the household of God.* Nairobi: Acton Publishers, 164-176.

Werline, R.A. 2014. Prayer, politics, and power in the Hebrew bible. *Interpretation: A journal of Bible and Theology* 68(1):5-16.

Willet, J., and Deegan, J.M. 2001. Liminality and disability: Rites of passage and community in hypermodern society. *Disability Studies Quarterly* 21(3):137-152.

Wikipedia. Female reproductive organs. https://en.wikipedia.org/wiki/ Female_reproductive_system. Accessed 12/12/15.

Wikipedia. Male reproductive organs. https://en.wikipedia.org/wiki/ Male_reproductive_system. Accessed 12/12/1

Wikipedia. The gizzard. https://en.wikipedia.org/wiki/Gizzard. Accessed 12/12/15.

ZDHS. 2007. Zambia. *2007 Demographic and health survey key findings.* http://www.measuredhs.com/pubs/pdf/SR157/SR157.pdf. Accessed 12/04/2011.

ENDNOTES

CHAPTER ONE

1. Victor W. Turner. 1967. The forest of symbols: Aspects of Ndembu ritual. Ithaca NY: Cornell University Press. Victor W. Turner. 1969. The ritual process: Structure and anti-structure. Chicago: Aldine.

2. Isabel Audrey Richards.1982. Chisungu: A girl's initiation ceremony among the Bembaof Zambia. London: Tavistock.

3. Richards. Chisungu, 120.

4. Richards. Chisungu, 123.

5. Richards. Chisungu, 123.

6. R. M. Kambole.1980. Ukufunda umwana kufikapo/Teach the child without beating about the bush. Lusaka: ZEPH.

7. Yizenge A. Chondoka. 1988. Traditional marriage in Zambia. Ndola: Mission Press.

8. Thera Rasing.1995. Passing on the rites of passage: Girls' initiation rites in the context of an urban Roman-Catholic community on the Zambian Copperbelt. Leiden: Avebury.

9. Rasing. Passing on the rites of passage, 5.

10. Rasing. Passing on the rites of passage, 7.

11. Rasing. Passing on the rites of passage, 7.

12. Rasing. Passing on the rites of passage, 17.

13. Mercy Oduyoye. 2004. Beads and Strands. Reflections of an African

woman on Christianity in Africa. Maryknoll: Orbis books, 80.

14. While both Islam and Christianity have contributed to the transformation of traditional African marriage and initiation rites, the present study will only focus on Christianity. This is because the history of colonialism in Central Africa and the history of Christianity are interlinked.

15. Isabel A. Phiri. 2000. Women, Presbyterianism and Patriarchy. Religious experiences of Chewa women in central Malawi. Blantyre: CLAIM.

16. Phiri. Women, Presbyterianism and Patriarchy, 62.

17. Molly Longwe. 2003. From Chinamwali to Chilangizo: the Christianisation of pre-Christian Chewa initiation rites in the Baptist convention of Malawi. Unpublished Masters Dissertation. University of KwaZulu-Natal.

18. Rachel Nyagondwe Fiedler. 2005. Coming of Age: A Christianised initiation for women in Southern Malawi. Zomba: Kachere.

19. Fiedler. Coming of Age, 12.

20. Fulata Moyo. 2009. A Quest for women's sexual empowerment through education in an HIV and AIDS context. Unpublished PhD Thesis. University of KwaZulu-Natal.

21. Moyo. A Quest for women's sexual empowerment, 5, 6.

22. Hugo Hinfelaar.1994. Bemba-speaking women of Zambia in a century of religious change (1892-1992). New York: Brill.

23. Hinfelaar. Bemba-speaking women of Zambia, 12.

24. Hinfelaar. Bemba-speaking women of Zambia, 29,180.

25. Chammah Kaunda. 2010. Reclaiming the feminine Image of God in Lesa. Implications for Bemba Christian women at the Evangel Assembly of God church in the post-missionary era. Journal of Constructive Theology 16(1):5-29.

26. Kaunda. Reclaiming the feminine image of God in Lesa, 26.

27. Augustus Kapungwe. 2003. Traditional cultural practices of imparting sex education and the fight against HIV/AIDS: The case of initiation ceremonies for girls in Zambia. African Sociological Review 7(1): 35-52, 37.

28. Lois Moyo. 2007. Widowhood rituals, African Lutherans and HIV prevention: A gendered study of the experiences of widows in the Kamwala Evangelical Lutheran church in Zambia. Unpublished Master's Thesis, 2-3.

Bridget Nonde Masaiti. 2007. African indigenous churches and polygamy in the context of HIV and AIDS: The case of the Mutima church in Zambia. Unpublished Master's Thesis, 5; Lillian Siwila. 2005. African women, hospitality and HIV/AIDS: The case of the mothers' union of St. Margaret's United Church of Zambia. Unpublished Master's thesis. University of KwaZulu-Natal.

29. Isabel Phiri and Sarojini Nadar. 2010. Talking back to religion and HIV and AIDS using an African Feminist missiological framework: Sketching the contours of the conversation. Journal of Constructive theology 16(2):8-24, 9.

30. Lillian Siwila. 2011b. Culture, gender, and HIV and AIDS: United Church of Zambia's response to traditional marriage practices. Unpublished PhD Thesis. University of KwaZulu-Natal.

31. Siwila. Culture, gender, and HIV and AIDS, 53, 82.

32. Siwila. Culture, gender, and HIV and AIDS, 194.

33. Beverley Haddad. 2008. Surviving the HIV and AIDS epidemic in South Africa: Women living and dying, Theologising and being theologised. Journal of Theology for Southern Africa 131(1): 47-57, 49.

34. Beverley Haddad. 2006. "We pray but we cannot heal": Theological challenges posed by the HIV/AIDS crisis. Journal of Theology for Southern Africa 125(1): 80-90, 89.

35. Isabel Phiri. 2003. African women of faith speak out in an HIV/AIDS era. In Phiri, I., Haddad, B., and Masenya, M. (eds.). African women, HIV/AIDS and faith communities. Pietermaritzburg: Cluster Publications, 3-20, 8-9.

36. Mushimbi Kanyoro. 2002. Introducing feminist cultural hermeneutics: An African perspective. Sheffield: Sheffield Academic Press, 18, 78.

37. Maaraidzo Mutambara. 2006. African women theologies critique inculturation. In Antonio Edward (ed.). Inculturation and post-colonial discourse in African theology. New York: Peter Lang, 173-186, 181.

38. Kanyoro. Introducing feminist cultural hermeneutics, 26.

39. D. Reeler. 2007. A three-fold theory of social change and implications for practice, planning, monitoring and evaluation. Cape Town: Centre for developmental practice, 1-33. T.C. Boas. 2007. Conceptualising

continuity and change: The composite-standard model of path dependence. Journal of theoretical politics 19(1):33-54, 33. K. Thelen. 2003. How institutions evolve: Insights from comparative historical analysis. In J. Mahoney and Ruschemeyer (eds.). Comparative historical analysis in the social sciences. New York: Cambridge University Press, 208-240.

40. Reeler. A three-fold theory of social change, 9. Kapambwe Lumbwe. 2013. Indigenous mfunkutu and contemporary ubwinga (wedding) music of the Bemba-speaking people of Zambia: Continuity and change. Journal of the musical arts in Africa 10:71-101, 73.

41. Jonathan, Kangwa. 2011. Reclaiming the values of female initiation rites as a strategy for HIV prevention: A gendered analysis of Chisungu initiation rites among the Bemba People of Zambia. MTh Thesis, University of KwaZulu-Natal; Lumbwe.Indigenous mfunkutu, 71-101.

42. Kangwa. Reclaiming the values of female initiation rites, Lumbwe. Indigenous mfunkutu, 71-101.

43. Philippe Dennis. 2000. Orality, memory and past: Listening to the voices of black clergy under colonialism and apartheid. Pietermaritzburg: Cluster Publications, 2.

44. Inculturation is a theological term which refers to a continuous process of dialogue between faith and culture. The process is motivated by, what Africans perceive to be, a situation of imbalance in the contact between African culture and Christianity as introduced into Africa by western missionaries (Ikechukwu 2008). The author of the present study perceives this imbalance as obstructing an unprejudiced take on the gendered cultural values of initiation rites.Benezet Bujo has shown that, while there are elements in traditional African culture that need to be challenged by the Christian gospel, the failure of western missionaries to distinguish between positive and negative elements in indigenous African culture was disastrous. For example, initiation rites which were central to religious and social structures in Africa were outright condemned. The same is true for African medicine. He argues that this stance of the missionaries destroyed the fabric of African culture and the opportunity of incarnating the Christian message in Africa was missed. Inculturation stresses Africa's religio-cultural realities. In this process, the contemporary African context should not be ignored. A theology which preaches the

necessity of inculturation but ignores the surrounding social misery, including oppression and HIV, is not life-giving. See Benezet Bujo. 1992. African theology in its social context. New York: Orbis, Emmanuel Martey. 1993. African theology. Inculturation and liberation. Maryknoll: Orbis.Inculturation is the intimate transformation of authentic cultural values through their integration in Christianity and the insertion of Christianity into African culture. By inculturation, the church makes the Gospel incarnate in African culture. The church assimilates African values which are not only compatible with the Gospel but also life-giving to people (Onsei-Bonsu 2005:20, Mutambara 2006:176). There must be a mutual and critical dialogue and integration. The Gospel on being introduced into any new region should not destroy that region's positive and life-giving cultural values. Inculturation involves a critical selection of elements from a given culture. The present study argues that those gendered cultural values that can be helpful in empowering women in the context of contemporary challenges need to be taken seriously by contemporary society. See Joseph Onsei-Bonsu. 2005. The inculturation of Christianity in Africa. Frankfurt am Main: Lang. Maaraidzo Mutambara. 2006. African women theologies critique inculturation. In Antonio Edward (ed.). Inculturation and post-colonial discourse in African theology. New York: Peter Lang, 173-186.

45. Fiedler. Coming of age, 45.

46. Fiedler. Coming of age, 29.

47. Hinfelaar. Bemba-speaking women of Zambia, 1,180.

48. Hinfelaar. Bemba-speaking women of Zambia, 180.

CHAPTER TWO

1. Fiedler. Coming of age, 5.

2. Jean La Fontaine. 1986. Initiation. Manchester: Manchester University Press, 11.

3. Victor W. Turner. 1982. Cerebration, studies in festivals and ritual. Washington: Smithsonian Institute Press, 105. Victor W. Turner. 1969. The ritual process: Structure and anti-structure. Chicago: Aldine.

4. A theory refers to a statement of general principles which try to

explain the nature of things. See Lucy W. Kibera and Agnes Kimoti. 2007. Fundamentals of sociology of education with reference to Africa. Nairobi: University of Nairobi Press, 13.

5.   Kibera W.L and Kimoti, A. 2007. Fundamentals of sociology of education with reference to Africa. Nairobi: University of Nairobi Press, 1.

6.   Kibera and Kimoti. Fundamentals of sociology of education, 2.

7.   Kibera and Kimoti. Fundamentals of sociology of education, 3.

8.   Kibera and Kimoti. Fundamentals of sociology of education, 4.

9.   Kibera and Kimoti. Fundamentals of sociology of education, 6.

10. Kibera and Kimoti. Fundamentals of sociology of education, 7.

11. Kibera and Kimoti. Fundamentals of sociology of education, 9.

12. Kibera and Kimoti. Fundamentals of sociology of education, 10.

13. Kibera and Kimoti. Fundamentals of sociology of education, 10.

14. Kibera and Kimoti. Fundamentals of sociology of education, 12.

15. Kibera and Kimoti. Fundamentals of sociology of education, 11-12. Marx Karl. 1884. The community manifesto. London: Penguin Books.

16. James F. Childress. 1986. Anthropology and ethics. In Childress, J.F., and Macquarrie, J. (eds). Dictionary of Christian ethics. London: SCM Press, 34-35.

17. Conrad P. Kottak. 2002. Anthropology: The exploration of human diversity. 9th edition. Boston: McGraw Hill, 27.

18. Kottak, Anthropology, 34.

19. Kottak, Anthropology, 15.

20. Kibera and Kimoti, 15.

21. Kottak. Anthropology, 4.

22. Kottak. Anthropology, 4.

23. Kottak. Anthropology, 488. Turner. The ritual process.

24. Kottak. Anthropology, 268.

25. Kottak. Anthropology, 5.

26. Kottak. Anthropology, 4.

27. Kottak. Anthropology, 11.

28. Kottak. Anthropology, 13.

29. Kottak. Anthropology, 281.

30. Kottak. Anthropology, 282.

31. Kottak. Anthropology, 276.

32. Kottak. Anthropology, 282.

33. Kottak. Anthropology, 276.

34. Bridge development-Gender report no. 55. http://www.bridge.ids.ac.uk/sites/bridge.ids.ac.uk/files/reports/re55.pdf. Accessed 01/01/16.

35. The words gender and sex are often used interchangeably. However, they are different in meaning. Sex refers to the biological features distinguishing males from females. Males and females differ in anatomy, hormones, and chromosomes. Gender refers to social, cultural, and psychological traits attached to males and females in society. In other words, sex makes one male or female while gender makes one masculine or feminine.

36. Kottak. Anthropology, 461.

37. Kottak. Anthropology, 460,462.

38. Kottak, Anthropology, 466.

39. Mercy Oduyoye. 1995. Daughters of Anowa. African women and patriarchy. Maryknoll: Orbis.

40. Kottak. Anthropology, 467.

41. Kottak. Anthropology, 469.

42. Linda Lindsey. 2011. Gender roles: A sociological perspective. 5th edition. New York: Pearson. 4. http://www.pearsonhighered.com/assets/hip/us/hip_us_pearsonhighered/samplechapter/0132448300.pdf. Accessed 16/12/15.

43. Lindsey. Gender roles, 2.

44. Lindsey. Gender roles, 3.

45. Lindsey. Gender roles, 3.

46. Lindsey. Gender roles, 3.

47. Lindsey. Gender roles, 4.

CHAPTER THREE

1. Rosemary Reuther cited in Susan Rakoczy. 2004. In her name: Women doing theology. Pietermaritzburg: Cluster Publications, 15. See also Rosemary Radford Reuther. 1993. Ecofeminism: Symbolic and social

connections of the oppression of women and domination of nature. In Adams, C.J. (ed.). Ecofeminism and the sacred. New York: Continuum, 13-23.

2. Kibera and Kimoti. Fundamentals of sociology, 44-45.

3. Rakoczy. In her name, 11.

4. Rakoczy. In her name, 11.

5. Rakoczy. In her name, 12.

6. Rakoczy. In her name, 13.

7. Rakoczy. In her name, 13.

8. Rakoczy. In her name, 13.

9. Rakoczy. In her name, 10.

10. Rakoczy. In her name, 11.

11. Rakoczy. In her name, 14.

12. See Sarojini Nadar. 2001. A South African Indian womanist reading of the character of Ruth. In Dube Musa (ed.). Other ways of reading. African women and the bible. Geneva: WCC publication.

13. Rakoczy. In her name, 6. Kibera and Kimoti. Fundamentals of sociology, 45.

14. Lindsey. Gender roles, 17.

15. Lindsey. Gender roles, 14.

16. Lindsey. Gender roles, 15.

17. Lindsey. Gender roles, 15. Kibera and Kimoti. Fundamentals of sociology, 46.

18. Lindsey. Gender roles, 15.

19. Kibera and Kimoti, 46.

20. Lindsey. Gender roles, 15.

21. Lindsey. Gender roles, 16.

22. Lindsey. Gender roles, 16.

23. Lindsey. Gender roles, 16.

24. Kibera and Kimoti. Fundamentals of sociology, 49.

25. Lindsey. Gender roles, 16.

26. Lindsey. Gender roles, 16.

27. Lindsey. Gender roles, 17.

28. Lindsey. Gender roles, 17.

29. Rosemary R. Ruether. 2011. Ecology and theology: Ecojustice at the

centre of church's mission. Interpretation (October): 355-365.

30. Ruether. Interpretation, 359.

31. A macro-sociological perspective on gender roles focuses on data collected on large-scale social phenomena such as labour force, educational, and political trends which are differentiated according to gender roles. Micro-sociological perspectives on gender roles focus on data collected in small groups such as couples and families.

32. Lindsey. Gender roles, 5.

33. Lindsey. Gender roles, 6.

34. Lindsey. Gender roles, 7-8.

35. Lindsey. Gender roles, 8.

36. Lindsey. Gender roles, 8.

37. Lindsey. Gender roles, 8-9.

38. Lindsey. Gender roles, 9.

39. Lindsey. Gender roles, 11.

40. Lindsey. Gender roles, 11.

41. Lindsey. Gender roles, 11.

42. Lindsey. Gender roles, 12.

43. Lindsey. Gender roles, 13.

44. Lindsey. Gender roles, 18.

45. Lindsey. Gender roles, 19.

46. Lindsey. Gender roles, 13.

47. Adrian S. van Klinken. 2011. Male headship as male agency: An alternative understanding of a 'patriarchal' African Pentecostal discourse on masculinity. Religion and Gender 1(1):104-124.

48. Van Klinken. Male headship as male agency, 104,114,120, 124.

49. Lindsey, Gender roles, 13.

CHAPTER FOUR

1. Rodney, A. Werline. 2014. Prayer, politics, and power in the Hebrew bible. Interpretation: A Journal of Bible and Theology 68(1): 2-16, 5.

2. Jeffrey Willet and Mary Jo Deegan. 2001. Liminality and disability: Rites of passage and community in hypermodern society. Disability Studies Quarterly 21(3):137-152.

3. Willet and Deegan. Liminality and disability.

4. Willet and Deegan. Liminality and disability.

5. Willet and Deegan. Liminality and disability. Turner. The forest of symbols, 93.

6. Willet and Deegan, Liminality and disability; Turner. The ritual process, 95.

7. Willet and Deegan. Liminality and disability.

8. Willet and Deegan. Liminality and disability.

9. Turner. The forest of symbols, 96-97.

10. Turner. The ritual process, 103.

11. Werline. Prayer and politics, 5.

12. Willet and Deegan. Liminality and disability, 137-152.

13. Werline. Prayer and politics, 6.

14. Werline. Prayer and politics, 6.

15. Werline. Prayer and politics. 7. See also Pierre Bourdieu. 1990. The logic of practice. Stanford: Stanford University Press, 3-65.

16. Cited in Werline. Prayer and politics, 5. See also Nathan D. Mitchell. 1999. Liturgy and the Social Sciences. Collegeville, MN: Liturgical, 88. Catherin Bell. 1992. Ritual theory, ritual practice. New York: Oxford University Press.

17. Bell rejects Marxist and Durkheimian claims that rituals are simply methods of control that mask power.

18. Cited in Werline. Prayer and politics, 7.

19. Arnold van Gennup.1960. The rites of passage. Trans. Monika B. Vizedom and Garbrielle L. Chicago: University of Chicago Press.

20. Werline. Prayer and politics, 10. See also Victor Turner. 1995. Ritual process: Structure and anti-structure. New York: de Gruyter, 94-130.

21. Werline. Prayer and politics, 10.See also Pierre Bourdieu. 2003. Language and symbolic power. Cambridge: Harvard University Press, 117-119.

22. Kottak. Anthropology, 495.

23. Kottak. Anthropology, 491.

24. Kottak. Anthropology, 495.

CHAPTER FIVE

1. Fiedler. Coming of age, 5.

2. La Fontaine. Initiation, 11.

3. Turner. Cerebration, 105.

4. Rasing. Passing on the rites of passage, 42. Richards. Chisungu, 123,125.

5. Turner Victor. 1981. Encounter with Freud. The making of a comparative symbologist. In Spindler G.D. (ed.). The meaning of a psychological anthropologist. California: University of California Press, 558-583. Rasing. Passing on the rites of passage, 35.

6. Richards. Chisungu, 128.

7. La Fontaine. Initiation, 104,116.

8. Rasing. Passing on the rites of passage, 41. Richards. Chisungu, 50.

9. Mercy Oduyoye. 1986. Hearing and knowing: Theological reflections on Christianity in Africa. New York: Orbis, 123.

10. In a matrilineal society, the married couple lives in the wife's village or compound and children trace their descent through the mother's line. A matriarchal society, therefore, gives a women high status and some freedom as compared to a patriarchal society. See Oduyoye 1995:134,135; Phiri 2000:35, 36).

11. Richards. Chisungu, 130.

12. Richards. Chisungu, 133.

13. Simon M. Kapwepwe. 1967. Shalapo canicandala / Goodbye old grass. Lusaka: ZEPH.

14. Central Statistical Office. 2011. Zambia census of population and housing: Parliamentary report. Lusaka: Central Statistical office.

15. Brian Garvey. 1994. Bembaland church: Religious and social change in South Central Africa, 1891-1964. New York: E.J Brill, 1.

16. Richards. Chisungu, 127.

17. Garvey. Bembaland church, 8.

18. Garvey Brian. Bembaland church, 11. Rasing. Passing on the rites of passage, 27.

19. Parkie Mbozi. 2000. The impact of negative cultural practices on the spread of HIV/AIDS in Zambia. Lusaka: UNZA, 80.

20. Richards. Chisungu, 49.

21. Garvey Brian. Bembaland church, 15.

22. La Fontaine. Initiation, 146.

23. Richards. Chisungu, 36.

24. Chammah Kaunda. 2010. Reclaiming the feminine Image of God in Lesa. Implications for Bemba Christian women at the Evangel Assembly of God Church inthe post-missionary era. Journal of Constructive Theology 16(1):5-29, 6.

25. Richards. Chisungu, 48.

26. Hinfelaar. Bemba-speaking women, 6, 7.

27. The Lunda people in Luapula province refer to Mukolo as Mwadi.

28. Richards. Chisungu, 49.

29. Mercy Oduyoye. 1986. Hearing and knowing: Theological reflections on Christianity in Africa. New York: Orbis, 183.

30. Richards. Chisungu, 110.

31. Rasing. Passing on the rites of passage, 31.

32. Richards. Chisungu, 56.

33. J.J. Corbeil. 1982. Mbusa: Sacred emblems of the Bemba. London: Ethnographic publishers, 9.

34. R. M. Kambole gives a full description of Chisungu initiation and Bemba traditional marriage. See Kambole, R M.1980. Ukufunda umwana kufikapo/Teach the child without beating about the bush. Lusaka: ZEPH.

35. There were variations to this component of the rites. If the initiate was not engaged, this part of the rites was performed during the marriage initiation ceremony. In any case the groom had to perform this ritual before the wedding ceremony.

36. There were different versions of this part of the ceremony. If the ceremony concerned the first menstruation of the bride, the groom would be invited to the bush where the Chisungu initiation ceremony was held. The initiation tutors asked him to jump over a small shrub of the mufungo tree while women beat drums, danced, and sang. The ritual was a kind of equivalent for jumping over the marriage emblem.

37. Cf. Elizabeth Cameron and Manuel Jordan. 2006. Playing with the future: children and rituals in North-Western province of Zambia. In Ottenberg, S., and Binkley, D. (eds.). African children masquerade. Playful

performers. London: Transaction Publishers, 237-246, 238.

38. Richards. Chisungu, 55.

39. Cf. Cameron and Jordan. Playing with the future, 238.

40. Rasing. Passing on the rites of passage, 52.

41. Addressing this issue may be a good starting point for teaching about the myths surrounding HIV and AIDS.

42. This could provide a useful resource in teachings on HIV prevention, for example, by abstinence and delaying the sex debut.

43. Richards. Chisungu, 51.

44. Rasing. Passing on the rites of passage, 6, 7.

45. Fiedler. Coming of Age, 31.

46. Isabel Phiri. 2003. African women of faith speak out in an HIV/AIDS era. In Phiri, I., Haddad, B., and Masenya, M. (eds.). African women, HIV/AIDS and faith communities. Pietermaritzburg: Cluster Publications, 3-20, 10.

47. Fiedler. Coming of age, 32.

48. Barbara Schmid. 2005. Sexuality and religion in the time of AIDS. Cape Town: ARSRC, 7.

49. Schmid. Sexuality and religion, 7.

50. Richards. Chisungu, 46.

51. Fiedler. Coming of age, 36.

52. Phiri. African women of faith, 10.

53. Rasing. Passing on the rites of passage, 6, 7.

54. Isabel Phiri. 2000b. 'Stand up and be counted: Identity, spirituality and theological education in my journey of faith'. In Denise Ackerman, Eliza Getman, Hantiecotze and Judy Tobler (eds). Claiming our footprints: South African women reflect on context, identity and spirituality. Stellenbosch: EFSA institute for theological and interdisciplinary research, 145-160, 150.

55. Fiedler. Coming of age, 47.

56. Cf. Kapungwe. Traditional cultural practices, 47.

CHAPTER SIX

1. La Fontaine. Initiation, 11.

2. Yizenge Chondoka and R.M Kambole have described Bemba traditional marriage in great detail. See Chondoka, Y.A. 1988.Traditional marriage in Zambia. Ndola: Mission Press. Kambole, R M.1980. Ukufunda umwana kufikapo/Teach the child without beating about the bush. Lusaka: ZEPH.

3. Richards. Chisungu, 128.

4. Richards. Chisungu, 130.

5. Engagement is also called ukusobola or ukusonga

6. Chondoka. Traditional marriage, 87.

7. Money here refers to anything of value which was used as a means of exchange. It could include hoes, a piece of cloth, beads, or a blanket.

8. R M. Kambole. 1974. Nkobekela te cupo/Engagement is not formal marriage. Lusaka: ZEPH.

9. If a girl has become engaged before puberty the second stage in the marriage process was Chisungu initiation. If she had already reached puberty the families proceeded directly to the food-offering ceremony.

10. After the explanation of the importance of a particular food item the father of the bride might take a small lump of nshima with a piece of chicken and feed the groom, thus ritually allowing him to eat any food in his house.

11. In some pre-colonial Bemba communities, wedding celebrations were opened by the initiation tutors who would give the groom a whip to whip the bride on the back. Should wife and husband fight, they should not involve the community. Also, the wife should not deny the husband sex just because they quarreled or fought. Sex should always be a privilege (kutombanafye).

12. See Kangwa. Reclaming the values of female initiation rites.

13. Among the Bemba of Luapula province of Zambia, the initiation rite prior to marriage includes the bride and the bridegroom having sex on the night before the wedding. This is to check whether the woman is a virgin or the man impotent (chibola). On this occasion, sexual intercourse between the engaged couple takes place on a bed covered with white linen. The tutors of initiation (ifimbusa) check the linen for the result of the coupling. In the same vein, the Chisungu ceremony incorporates aspects of virginity and virility inspection.

14. Kambole. Ukufunda umwana.

15. In some communities this ritual was performed in the evening after the gifting ceremony (ukuluula).

16. In modern days a small dish is used.

17. See Lumbwe, Kapambwe. 2013. Indigenous mfunkutu and contemporary ubwinga (wedding) music of the Bemba-speaking people of Zambia: Continuity and change. Journal of the musical arts in Africa 10:71-101, 78.

CHAPTER SEVEN

1. Cameron and Jordan. Playing with the future, 238.
2. Kanyoro. Introducing feminist cultural hermeneutics, 19.
3. Hinfelaar. Bemba-speaking women, xi.
4. Hinfelaar. Bemba-speaking women, 3.
5. Rasing. Passing on the rites of passage, 51, 52.
6. Kaunda. Reclaiming the feminine image of God, 7.
7. Hinfelaar. Bemba-speaking women, 6.
8. Karla Poewe. 1981. Matrilineal ideology. Male and female dynamics in the Luapula, Zambia. London: Academic Press Inc, 56.
9. Rackozy. In Her name, 63.
10. Poewe. Matrilineal ideology, 56-57; M. Douglas. 1966: Purity and danger: An analysis of the concepts of pollution and taboo: London: Routledge, 157.
11. Rasing. Passing on the rites of passage, 28.
12. Oduyoye. Daughters of Avowal, 176.
13. Hinfelaar. Bemba-speaking women, 11.
14. Richards. Chisungu, 50.
15. Hinfelaar. Bemba-speaking women, 12.
16. Rasing. Passing on the rites of passage, 27.
17. Hinfelaar. Bemba-speaking women, 13.
18. Rasing. Passing on the rites of passage, 29.
19. Garvey. Bembaland church, 11.
20. Hinfelaar. Bemba-speaking women, 15.
21. Richards, Chisungu, 139.

22. Hinfelaar. Bemba-speaking women, 17.

23. Richards. Chisungu, 61.

24. Richards. Chisungu, 59.

25. Richards. Chisungu, 75.

26. Hinfelaar. Bemba-speaking women, 15.

27. Richards. Chisungu, 94.

28. Rasing. Passing on the rites of passage, 55.

29. Richards. Chisungu, 103.

30. Richards. Chisungu, 87. Rasing. Passing on the rites of passage, 66.

31. Richards. Chisungu, 210.

32. Richards. Chisungu, 104. Rasing. Passing on the rites of passage, 60.

33. Richards. Chisungu, 50.

34. Richards. Chisungu, 83.

35. Rasing. Passing on the rites of passage, 69.

36. Rasing. Passing on the rites of passage, 71. Richards. Chisungu, 83.

37. Rasing. Passing on the rites of passage, 72.

38. Peggy M. Kabonde. 1996. Widowhood in Zambia: The effects of ritual. In Kanyoro, M. and Njoroge, N. (eds.). Groaning in faith. African women in the household of God. Nairobi: Acton Publishers, 197.

39. Rasing. Passing on the rites of passage, 70.

40. Corbeil. Mbusa, 17. La Fontaine. Initiation, 103.

41. La Fontaine Jean. 1982. Introduction. In Richards, Audrey. Chisungu: A girl's initiation ceremony among the Bemba of Zambia. London: Tavistock, xvii-xxxvii, xxxi.

42. Fiedler. Coming of age, 19.

43. Female reproductive system. https://en.wikipedia.org/wiki/Female_reproductive_system. Accessed 12/12/15.

44. Female reproductive system. https://en.wikipedia.org/wiki/Female_reproductive_system. Accessed 12/12/15.

45. Reproductive Organs. http://www.healthline.com/human-body-maps/female-reproductive-organs. Accessed 12/12/15.

46. Male Reproductive system (diagram). http://patient.info/diagram/male-reproductive-system-diagram. Accessed 12/12/15.

47. Wikipedia. Gizzard. https://en.wikipedia.org/wiki/Gizzard.

48. S J. Guedes. 2006. Bali fye umubili umo: Amafundisho ya cupo.

Ndola: Mission Press, 149.

49. Guedes. Balifye umubili umo, 152, 153.

50. Rasing. Passing on the rites of passage, 55.

51. Richards. Chisungu, 192.

52. Rasing. Passing on the rites of passage, 81.

53. Richards. Chisungu, 85,196.

54. Richards. Chisungu, 189.

55. Richards. Chisungu, 198.

56. Rasing. Passing on the rites of passage, 78.

57. Kabonde. Widowhood in Zambia, 192.

CHAPTER EIGHT

1. La Fontaine. Introduction, xxv.

2. Rasing. Passing on the rites of passage, 26.

3. Phiri. Stand up and be counted, 150.

4. Kapungwe. Traditional cultural practices, 38.

5. Richards. Chisungu, 115.

6. To demythologize is to remove the mysterious and mythical aspects which are life denying to women. Christina Landman has suggested that in liberating women, we need to demystify and deconstruct myths surrounding sexuality and the physical bodies of women. See Landman Christina. 1998. African women's theologies. In maimela and Konic (eds.). Initiation into theology: The varieties of theology and hermeneutics. Pretoria: J.L. Van Schalk publishers, 137-140,138.

7. Kapungwe. Traditional cultural practices, 45.

8. La Fontaine. Introduction, xxxiv.

9. Mercy Oduyoye. 2004. Beads and strands. Reflections of an African woman on Christianity in Africa. Maryknoll: Orbis books, 87. Wamwue, Grace. 1996. Women and taboo among the Kikuyu people. In Kanyoro, M. and Njoroge, N. (eds.). Groaning in faith. African women in the household of God. Nairobi: Acton Publishers, 164-176,172.

10. Oduyoye. Beads and trands, 87.

11. Oduyoye. Beads and strands, 85.

12. Kurian Manoj. 2004. "The HIV and AIDS pandemic changing

perceptions on sexuality in faith communities". Ecumenical Review 56(4): 432-436,432.

13. Mbozi. The impact of negative cultural practices, 80. Moyo. A quest for women's sexual empowerment, 11.

14. Haddad. Choosing to remain silent, 151. Moyo. A quest for women's sexual empowerment, 16.

15. Richards. Chisungu, 50.

16. Moyo. A quest for women's sexual empowerment, 11,112.

17. Rasing. Passing on the rites of passage, 70.

18. To demythologize means to deconstruct and demystify myths surrounding marriage and fertility (Landman 1998:138).

19. Rasing. Passing on the rites of passage, 26. Mercy Oduyoye. 1999. A coming home to myself. The childless woman in the West African space. In Farley, Margaret, and Jones, Serene (eds.). Liberating eschatology. Essays in honour of Letty M. Russell. Louisville: Westminster John Knox Press, 113.

20. Rasing. Passing on the rites of passage, 32.

21. Gnanadason, A. 1993. No longer a secret: The church and violence against women. Geneva: WCC publications, 8.

22. Oduyoye. A coming home to myself, 114,116.

23. Masenya Madipoane. 2003. Trapped between two "canons": African-South African Christian women in the HIV/AIDS era. In Phiri, Isabel et al (eds.). African women, HIV/AIDS and faith communities. Pietermaritzburg: Cluster Publications, 113-127,123.

24. La Fontaine. Introduction, xxxiv.

25. Rasing. Passing on the rites of passage, 72.

26. Mbozi. The impact of negative cultural practices, 80.

27. Bah, Ida. 2005. Gender inequality and HIV/AIDS in Zambia: A study of the links between gender inequality and women's vulnerability to HIV/AIDS. Huddinge: ISNJ, 32.

28. Fiedler, Klaus. 1996. Christianity and African culture. Conservative German protestant missionaries in Tanzania, 1900-1940. Leiden: Brill, 180.

29. Haddad. Choosing to remain silent, 151. Philippe Denis. 2003. Sexuality and AIDS in Southern Africa. Journal of theology for Southern Africa 113(March):63-77, 90. Phiri. African women of faith, 11.

30. Haddad. Choosing to remain silent, 151.

31. Phiri. African women of faith, 10.

32. La Fontaine. Introduction, xvii.

33. Touwen, A. 1984. "I'm suffering". A pilot study of the position of female heads-of- households in a rural Copperbelt community in Zambia. Groningen: University of Groningen, 38.

34. Poewe. Matrilineal ideology, 55.

35. Epstein, A.L. 1981. Urbanisation and kinship: The domestic domain on the Copperbelt of Zambia 1950-1956. London: Academic Press, 68, 70.

36. Bah. Gender inequality, 1. Siwila. Problematising a 'norm', 42.

37. Rasing. Passing on the rites of passage, 30. Kaunda. Reclaiming the feminine image, 6.

38. Kaunda. Reclaiming the feminine image, 6.

39. Kaunda. Reclaiming the feminine image, 5.

40. Kaunda. Reclaiming the feminine Image, 6.

41. Kaunda. Reclaiming the feminine Image, 7.

42. Hinfelaar. Bemba speaking women, 192.

43. Kaunda. Reclaiming the feminine image, 12.

44. Moyo, A quest for women's sexual empowerment, 75.

45. Reuther, Rosemary. 1983. Sexism and God-talk: Towards a feminist theology. London: SCM Press, 53.

46. Kaunda. Reclaiming the feminine image, 25.

47. Rakoczy. In her name, 63.

48. Moyo. A quest for women's sexual empowerment, 75.

49. Masaiti. African indigenous churches, 83.

50. Jane L. Parpart. 1994. Where is your mother?: Gender, urban marriage, and colonial discourse on the Zambian Copperbelt, 1924-1945. The International Journal of African Historical Studies 27(2):241-271.

51. La Fontaine. Initiation, 146.

52. La Fontaine. Initiation, 164.

53. Rasing. Passing on the rites of passage, 78. Corbeil. Mbusa, 17.

54. Hinfelaar. Bemba-speaking women, 194.

55. Maluleke Tinyiko. 2001. African "Ruths", Ruthless Africa: Reflections of an African Modecai. In Musa, Dube (ed.). Other ways of reading. African women and the bible. Geneva: WCC Publications, 238.

56. Haddad, Beverley. Choosing to remain silent, 155.

57. Phiri Isabel and Nadar, Sarojini. 2010. Talking back to religion and HIV and AIDS using an African feminist missiological framework: Sketching the contours of the conversation. Journal of Constructive Theology 16(2):8-24,10.

58. Siwila. Problematising a 'norm', 38. Oduyoye. Beads and strands, 80.

59. Bruce, Patricia. 2003. "The mother's cow": A study of Old Testament references to virginity in the context of HIV/AIDS in South Africa. In Phiri, I, Haddad, B., and Masenya, M. (eds.). African women, HIV, AIDS and faith communities. Pietermaritzburg: Cluster Publication, 53.

60. Bruce. The mother's cow, 46.

61. Bruce. The mother's cow, 53.

62. Bruce. The mother's cow, 64.

63. Gomes, Eva. 1996. Sexuality and the well-being of women. In Kanyoro, M. and Njoroge, N. (eds.). Groaning in faith. African women in the household of God. Nairobi: Acton Publishers, 226.

64. Phiri, Isabel. 2006. Dealing with the trauma of sexual abuse. A gender-based analysis of the testimonies of female traditional healers in KwaZulu-Natal. In Phiri, Isabel and Nadar, Sarojini (eds.). African women, religion and health. Essays in honour of Mercy Amba Ewudzima Oduyoye. Pietermaritzburg: Cluster Publications, 113-130,126.

65. Bruce. The mother's cow, 67.

66. Abigail Harrison. 2005. Young people and HIV/AIDS in South Africa: prevalence of infection, risk factors and social context. Cambridge: Cambridge New Press, 22,29.

CHAPTER NINE

1. Garvey. Bembaland church, 10.

2. Denis Philippe. 2003. Sexuality and AIDS, 67.

3. Masenya. Trapped between two canons, 119.

4. Phiri, Isabel. 1997. Doing theology in the community: The case of African women theologians in the 1990s. Journal of theology for southern Africa 99:68-76, 72.

5.   Unlike the protestant churches, the Roman-Catholic church in Zambia has inculturated marriage and female initiation rites. See Jose dos Santos Guedes. 2006. Bali fye umubili umo: Amafundisho ya cupo. Ndola: Mission Press. Hinfelaar. Bemba-speaking women of Zambia, 191,192.

6.   UCZ Synod. 2008. Minutes of the 24th synod meeting of the United Church of Zambia held at Diakonia centre, Kabwe, from 1st to 6th June 2008, 22.

7.   Kanyoro. Engendered communal theology, 161. Kanyoro. Introducing feminist cultural hermeneutics, 18.

8.   Kanyoro. Engendered communal theology, 167.

9.   Martey. African theology, 67.

10. Onsei-Bonsu, Joseph. The inculturation, 19.

11. Onsei-Bonsu, Joseph. The inculturation, 19.

12. Onsei-Bonsu, Joseph. The inculturation, 122.

13. Kaunda, Chammah. 2010b. Creation as a dwelling place of God: A critical analysis of an African biocentric theology in the works of Gabriel M. Sotiloane. Unpublished Master's thesis. University of Kwa Zulu-Natal, 9.

14. Kanyoro. Engendered communal theology, 167. Mutambara. African women theologies, 180.

15. Rasing.Passing on the rites of passage, 2.

16. Longwe. From Chinamwali to Chilangizo, 136.

17. Longwe. From Chinamwali to Chilangizo, 136.

18. Longwe. From Chinamwali to Chilangizo, 136.

19. Moyo. A quest for women's sexual empowerment, 243.

20. Peter Bolink. 1967. Towards church union in Zambia. A study of missionary co-operation and church union efforts in central Africa. Franeker: T. Wever, 363. UCZ constitution, 1.

21. Bolink. Towards church union in Zambia, 363. Siwila, Lillian. Problematising a 'norm', 33.

22. L.M. Orger. 1991. "Where a scattered flock gathered". Ilondola. Ndola. Mission Press, 199.

23. Rotberg, Robert. 1965. Christian missionaries and the creation of Northern Rhodesia 1880-1924. Princeton: Princeton University Press, 39, 40. Hinfelaar. Bemba-speaking women, 37,60.

24. See Julia Allen. 2008. Mabel Shaw's theology in the context of her work as a Christian missionary teacher in Northern Rhodesia, 1915-1940. Feminist Theology 16(2): 194-210.

25. Bujo. African theology, 44, 45.

26. Garvey. Bembaland church, 177,178.

27. Hinfelaar. Bemba-speaking women, 154,155.

28. Rasing. Passing on the rites of passage, 2.

29. Rasing. Passing on the rites of passage, 22.

30. Phiri, Isabel. Stand up and be counted, 150.

31. Phiri, Isabel. Stand up and be counted, 150.

32. UCZ HIV/AIDS policy. 2006. Synod community development department of the united church of Zambia. Lusaka, Zambia, 14.

33. UCZ HIV/AIDS policy, 5-12.

34. UCZ HIV/AIDS policy, 12, 15.

35. Siwila Lillian. Problematising a 'norm', 36; Siwila. Culture, Gender, and HIV and AIDS, 51.

36. Johannes Heath. 2009. The need for comprehensive multi-faceted interventions. Geneva: EAA, 72.

37. Van Klinken, Adriaan. 2011. Transforming masculinities towards gender justice in an era of HIV and AIDS. Plotting the pathways. In Haddad, Beverley (ed.). Religion and HIV and AIDS. Charting the terrain. Pietermaritzburg: UKZN Press, 291.

38. Schmid. Sexuality and religion, 7, 8.

39. Siwila, Lillian. Problematising a 'norm', 36.

40. Siwila, Lillian. Problematising a 'norm', 42.

41. Moyo. A quest for women's sexual empowerment, 122.

42. Masenya Madipoane. 2010. All from the same source? Deconstructing a (male) anthropocentric reading of Job (3) through an eco-bosadi lens. Journal of Theology for Southern Africa 137 (July): 46-60, 51. Kaunda. Reclaiming the feminine image, 6-7; Kaunda, Chammah. 2010b. Creation as a dwelling place of God: A critical analysis of an African biocentric theology in the works of Gabriel M. Sotiloane. Unpublished Master's thesis. University of KwaZulu-Natal, 1.

43. Moyo. A quest for women's sexual empowerment, 127.

44. Fiedler. Christianity and African culture, 198.

45. Moyo. A Quest for women's sexual empowerment, 123.

46. Landman. African women's theologies, 138.

47. Siwila. Culture, Gender, and HIV and AIDS, 124.

48. Fiedler. Coming of age, 43-44.

CHAPTER TEN

1. Hinfelaar. Bemba-speaking women, 165.

2. Personal communication with Rev. Charles Lungu, minister of the United Church of Zambia, Riverside Congregation in Kitwe on 14 April 2012.

3. Landman. African women's theologies, 138,139.

4. Lumbwe, Indigenous mfunkutu, 73.

5. Lumbwe. Indigenous mfunkutu, 71.

6. Lumbwe. Indigenous mfunkutu, 71.

7. Kapungwe. Traditional cultural practices, 35.

8. UNAIDS 2009 update http://www.unaids.org/en/ knowledgecentre/HIVData/Epiupdate/EpiupdArc. Accessed 04/08/2011.

9. UNAIDS 2010 update. http://www.unaids.org/en/media/unaids/ contentassets/documents/unaidspublication/2010/20101123_globalref. Accessed 22/5/11.

10. MOH/NAC. 2010. Zambia country report. Monitoring the Declaration of commitment on HIV and AIDS and the Universal access. Submitted to the United Nations General Assembly special session on AIDS declaration of commitment on 31/03/10, 24.

11. UNAIDS 2010 update. http://www.unaids.org/en/media/unaids/ contentassets/documents/unaidspublication/2010/20101123_globalref. Accessed 22/5/11.

12. MOH/NAC. 2010. Zambia country report, 25.

13. MOH/NAC. 2010. Zambia country report, 25.

14. ZDHS. 2007. Zambia. 2007 Demographic and Health survey key findings. http://www.measuredhs.com/pubs/pdf/SR157/SR157.pdf, 22.

15. Moyo, Fulata. 2005. Sex, gender, power and HIV/AIDS in Malawi: Threats and challenges to women being church. In Phiri and Nadar (eds). On being church: African women's voices and visions. Geneva: WCC, 127-

145, 130.

16. Kapungwe. Traditional cultural practices, 35.

17. Phiri and Nadar. Talking back to religion,19.

18. R.M. Kambole. 1980. Ukufunda umwana kufikapo/Absolute marriage titbits. Lusaka: ZEPH.

19. Kottak. Anthropology, 460.

20. Kambole. Ukufunda umwana, 17.

21. Kambole. Ukufunda umwana, 16-17.

22. Kambole. Ukufunda umwana, 16-17.

23. Kambole. Ukufunda umwana, 16-17.

24. Kambole. Ukufunda umwana, 16-17.

25. Kambole. Ukufunda umwana, 17.

26. Anderson, Ben. 2007. The politics of homosexuality in Africa. Africana 1:123-136, 126

27. Lumbwe. Indigenous mfunkutu, 73. Boas. Conceptualising continuity and change, 3. Reeler. A three-fold theory of social change, 10-17. Thelen. How institutions evolve.

28. Boas. Conceptualising continuity and change, 33. Lumbwe. Indigenous mfunkutu, 73.

29. Lumbwe. Indigenous mfunkutu, 73-74. cf. D. Leat. 2005. Theories of social change: background paper. In The INSP theory of change tool manual. Washington: International Network on Strategic Philanthropy, 1-16.

30. Marriage blessings can also take place at the civic centre if its marriage by ordinance or at any places chosen by the family if its traditional marriage.

31. Kapungwe. Traditional cultural practices, 45.

32. Kottak. Anthropology, 477.

33. Kottak. Anthropology, 477.

CHAPTER ELEVEN

1. S. D. Taylor. 2006. Culture and customs of Zambia. London: Greenwood Press, 92.

2. Taylor. Culture and customs, 92.

3. Taylor. Culture and customs, 92.

www.ingramcontent.com/pod-product-compliance
Lightning Source LLC
Chambersburg PA
CBHW071149290526
45788CB00001BA/198